NEWCASTLE UNITED
MINUTE
BY MINUTE

NEWCASTLE UNITED
MINUTE
BY MINUTE

Covering More Than 500 Goals,
Penalties, Red Cards and
Other Intriguing Facts

DAVID JACKSON

First published by Pitch Publishing, 2020

Pitch Publishing
A2 Yeoman Gate
Yeoman Way
Worthing
Sussex
BN13 3QZ
www.pitchpublishing.co.uk
info@pitchpublishing.co.uk

© 2020, David Jackson

A CIP catalogue record is available for this book
from the British Library.

ISBN 978 1 78531 664 7

Typesetting and origination by Pitch Publishing
Printed and bound by TJ International, Padstow, UK

Contents

Dedicated to ...

*Supermac – a genuine United legend –
and to the memory of Gary Speed*

Acknowledgements

Newcastle United: Minute by Minute was a hard book to research – a very hard book – but thanks to certain resources, websites and media outlets, it was made a lot easier.

The goal times are taken from various resources and, whenever possible, Opta – but also BBC match reports, Sky Sports reruns, *Match of the Day*, endless YouTube highlights of games that would have otherwise been impossible to describe (and countless newspaper clippings and old match reports that sometimes tested my eyesight to the limit), plus Newcastle United FC's official website and various other fan sites and stats platforms such as Soccerbase, Transfermarkt and 11v11.

But a huge thanks to the guys who run nufc.com – an absolute treasure trove of stats and facts from years gone by that I discovered about halfway through writing this book – they had crucial dates and, more importantly, goal times of goals that I knew of, but where I couldn't find reports of the matches for love nor money. An absolutely brilliant website that every stat-mad United fan should cherish.

I'd also like to thank Magpies legend Malcolm Macdonald for very kindly providing the foreword for this book. 'Supermac' had reached legendary status at St James' Park long before manager Gordon Lee – with whom he had a famously fractious relationship – made it clear he should perhaps seek pastures new. His goals per game record was phenomenal and I feel sure he would have gone on to have broken numerous scoring records for the Magpies have had he been able to play two or three more seasons. He is still adored on Tyneside and lives in the city to this day. He was a pleasure to talk to and I thank him for his time and entertaining recollections of his time with the club. What a legend.

What I will say is this – the book you are about to read has been thoroughly researched and has in excess of 500 goals which – apart from a handful that were impossible to find footage of – I have viewed and then described in bite-sized detail. If there is the odd one where the player stated as making the final pass or cross is incorrect, it will be because his shirt number or image was difficult to make out. There may be one or two, but I'm certain 99.9 per cent are accurate!

One thing I learned was that this football club has had many thrilling periods, such as the arrival of Kevin Keegan as a player – and then a manager – and the hysteria that surrounded those eras; the arrival of favourite son Alan Shearer and the incredible career he enjoyed in black and white; not forgetting the dignity and joy of Sir Bobby Robson's stint as boss and even the exciting Magpies side that thrilled the Premier League under Alan Pardew in 2011/12. As I write, the United fans are waiting to see if a takeover has been completed in time for the post-COVID-19 2020/21 campaign.

When Newcastle United get momentum behind them, there is no stopping the club or its supporters and an exciting new era feels tantalisingly close.

ACKNOWLEDGEMENTS

Finally, I'd like to thank my wife and kids for being patient during the many hours I have invested in this project, and Paul and Jane Camillin – the tireless siblings who mastermind the very brilliant Pitch Publishing – for green-lighting this series. It's been on Paul's radar for three or four years and finally, we have an end result ...

Introduction

In a unique first, *Newcastle United: Minute by Minute* takes you through the Magpies' matchday history and records the historic goals, incidents and memorable moments and the minute they happened in.

From United's glorious early years and domestic domination through to the present day, this is a comprehensive listing of every memorable moment during matches and the minute it occurred in. From Frank Watt's early trophy-hunters to Stan Seymour's FA Cup legends, from Kevin Keegan's swashbuckling Entertainers through to Sir Bobby Robson's excellent Magpies side and, of course, the Alan Shearer years.

You will also discover a crucial goal has so often been scored at the same minute so often over the years – and how some minutes (such as eight) feature far less for some reason. From goals scored in the opening few seconds to the last-gasp extra-time winners that have thrilled generations of fans at St James' Park, or United fans (for they are legion) around the world.

Newcastle United: Minute by Minute has it all, with countless goals from the legendary Alan Shearer, Jackie Milburn, Malcolm Macdonald, David Ginola, Andy Carroll, Ayoze Perez, Papiss Cisse – even David Batty – and hundreds of others.

Howay the lads!

Foreword

By Malcolm Macdonald (1971–76)
Appearances: 257 Goals: 138

26, 44 and 67

For a book on minutes when Newcastle United goals were scored, those three particular goal times will be forever etched in my memory as they are, as some of you might have already guessed, the times of my three goals against Liverpool on my home debut.

It was almost 50 years ago now, but I still remember that game as though it was yesterday.

The day in question began when Bobby Moncur, the captain of the team, asked me, David Craig and Frank Clark along to sit with him at a signing session of a book he'd just released – *United We Stand* – at Waterstones and maybe sign a few copies for fans as well. It was late Saturday morning and, when we'd finished, we went to a nearby restaurant to have eggs on toast and suchlike as our pre-match meal before making our way up to the ground for our game against Liverpool.

This was my first experience of playing in front of a massive crowd because my previous two clubs – Fulham and Luton Town – were used to playing in front of less than 10,000 in the lower divisions and, dear me, when I got to St James' Park it was absolutely heaving. I parked my car near the stadium and, within a minute or two, there were maybe 200 local kids crowding around asking for an autograph. I looked at my watch and knew that if I started signing I'd be there until after kick-off, so I promised I would do it, but after the game and, though they were disappointed, they knew I meant it and so I made my way to the stadium entrance, up the steps and inside.

Liverpool were one of the top teams at the time, along with Leeds United and Arsenal, and as we were near the foot of the table, this was a huge game for us and, in truth, one we were expected to lose. At St James' Park, you have to go down some steps to get to the level of the pitch and then it's about a ten-yard walk to the end of the tunnel, and as I took each step the noise grew louder until reaching a crescendo as we stepped out on to the pitch. I'd never experienced anything like it.

I'd already played for Newcastle twice by that point, but both games had been away – a 2-0 defeat at Crystal Palace where we played like a bunch of strangers, and then against Spurs where there was a noticeable improvement. There was Terry Hibbitt, Paddy Howard and me who had all arrived at the club and we hadn't gelled at Selhurst Park, but there was definite reason for encouragement at White Hart Lane. That was the second game of the season and yet, in between the Crystal Palace and Tottenham games, the referees had been told to clamp down on certain infringements and fouls, and the Spurs game was something of a wake-up call for everyone because the ref booked Mike England for a tackle on me from behind and he said, 'Ref, if you're going to book me for that, I'm going to be out of a job!'

Then Joe Kinnear went to pick up the ball for a throw-in but, as he did, the linesman's flag went up and the referee blew and said the ball hadn't gone out and took his name as well! It seemed all the understanding between players and officials we'd had before had gone out of the window. Still, we got a 0-0 draw and we were happy enough.

Bear in mind I had just signed from Luton and both games had been down in London, so walking into St James' Park was a different world and it was the Newcastle supporters' first real look at me. It was literally deafening, the place was heaving and I suppose it could have frightened the life out of me, but we are all different and some players get nervous and some thrive on that kind of atmosphere – I absolutely loved it and it got my adrenaline pumping and I couldn't have been happier. I quickly discovered I loved setting the crowd off and really getting them pumped up.

So on my home debut, we went a goal down to Liverpool through Emlyn Hughes, who was playing in midfield at the time, and he ran back to the halfway line doing that crazy dance celebration of his as he always did. Then, we hit back. There was a lad in the side that day called David Young and he may not have lasted very long at the club, but he helped me get my first goal. He made a clever run into the Liverpool box and, as he went past Kevin Keegan, he tripped him – thanks Kevin – and that gave me the chance to score my first goal from the penalty spot. I felt confident, ran up and thumped it high into the top-left corner – which was just as well because Ray Clemence guessed the right way and would have saved it had it been any lower.

I was by now beginning to learn what a super little player Terry Hibbitt was. He had a wonderful left peg and was a very clever footballer. I'd had a few games at Fulham as a lad with the pass master that was Johnny Haynes and I would put Hibbitt in the same bracket with the only caveat being Haynes was naturally two-footed whereas Terry used his right for standing on only!

Hibby has the ball on the inside-left position and I've made a run to the left of the box, and what he used to do was play a pass so the defender would have to commit himself and all it needed was for the recipient to have a couple of yards' sprint to be able to nick it past and you were away. On this occasion, the defender was Larry Lloyd and, just as he was about to come in and clear it, I nicked it off his toe on the left side of the box and went around him and then cracked it as hard as I could into the far top-right corner of the net to make it 2-1.

One of the most remarkable things that I've ever experienced took place in the seconds that followed that goal. I'd gone running to the corner flag on the left to celebrate with the fans and my team-mates and, as we ran back to the halfway line to kick off again, the whole of St James' Park (bar the Liverpool contingent) started singing to the tune of the hit musical theme from *Jesus Christ Superstar,* which was huge at the time. They sang, 'Supermac, superstar, how many goals have you scored so far?' They all sang together in unison and it was a bit special, but I was wondering if there had been song sheets handed out in preparation! I just thought, 'This is wonderful, a fantastic place full of very special people.' Something magical took place at that moment between me and the fans and it's why I've lived all my life since in the north-east. The people up here are just different class.

And my day just kept getting better. After half-time, Hibbitt, by now running the show, picked up the ball on the left inside our own half and then just ran at the Liverpool defence – and ran, and ran – while Liverpool's defence were trying to get back. John Tudor and I had started to forge a real understanding and, as he ran one way, I ran the other and Hibby plays a pass into Tudor and instead of controlling it, he just flicked it on for me running in just behind and I buried a low shot past Clemence to complete a hat-trick, on my home debut against one of the best sides in the country.

It was an incredible start to life at St James' Park, but sadly, my afternoon ended not long after.

Clemence was such a sweet striker of a football and could ping it wherever he wanted, but on this occasion he duffed it along the ground and I can only think he did it purposely. It went past Lloyd and came to me but it bobbled a bit as I went to control it and it struck my ankle and went up in the air. I sprinted after it, past Larry Lloyd towards the Liverpool box, and I see Clemence rushing out, looking at me in the eye. I looked for the ball which was coming down and instantly knew I didn't have time for it to land so leapt up off my feet and lobbed it over Clemence towards goal and, as I landed, I looked over the shoulder over the advancing Clemence and see it drops on top of the roof of the net ... just as I get clattered in the side of the face with the studs of Clemence's size nine left boot. Dear me, it did some damage! It split all of my upper lip on the left-hand side and it was a huge gash. I was struggling to maintain consciousness and the game was stopped while the physio and trainer came on. They wanted to stretcher me off, but I said no to the stretcher and instead they both helped me off, but I could barely walk as my legs had gone and I'd been completely wiped out.

When I did get in the changing rooms, I lay on one of the physio beds and actually did fall unconscious. The next thing I knew, Frank Clark was stood at the end of the physio bed – now let me quickly put something in context because Malcolm Macdonald being asleep on one of those beds was not uncommon! I was so relaxed before a match that I would sometimes have a ten-minute power nap on there, so when I came around, I was groggy and confused and just thought I must have had a quick nap before the game. I said to him, 'Is it time to go out for the game, Frank?'

He just smiled and said: 'Bonny lad, what are you talking about? The game's over, we've won 3-2 and you've scored a hat-trick!' I couldn't believe it and, at that moment, had no recollection of what had happened that afternoon, but fortunately, Tyne Tees TV had been there and I was able to watch the game the following day and enjoy it all over again.

I went on to be the top scorer in all five of my seasons on Tyneside and averaged around 27.5 goals per season, which I think is still a record for Newcastle United on a goals per game basis. It was the happiest time of my career and the fact the supporters are still as fantastic with me today as they were back then is the reason I'll never stray too far from this city.

So, those were three of my special minutes in black and white, though the truth is they were all special. Now, enjoy hundreds more memorable moments that have happened in Newcastle United's long and proud history ... and yes, there are a couple more of my more memorable efforts for the club in there somewhere.

Malcolm Macdonald, Newcastle, 2020

Newcastle United: Minute by Minute

The clock is ticking ...
Howay the lads!

First half

5 seconds

29 July 1972

Malcolm Macdonald scores what is believed to be Newcastle United's fastest-ever goal in a pre-season friendly at Muirton Park against St Johnstone. Supermac spots the keeper off his line just prior to kick-off and, as the referee blows his whistle, the ball is nudged to him by John Tudor to get the game underway and Supermac immediately thumps a powerful 50-yard-plus shot over the keeper's head and into the net without touching the ground. With just five seconds played, it was an incredible goal and, not only that, one of the fastest strikes of all time.

11 seconds

18 January 2003

Alan Shearer equals the Premier League record for the fastest goal scored as he gets the Magpies off to a flying start against Kevin Keegan's Manchester City. In what is Keegan's first top-flight return to St James' Park after leaving the club six years earlier, the warm reception he received was soon replaced by the majority of the 52,152 crowd celebrating as City keeper Carlo Nash's early touch and attempted clearance is charged down by Shearer who then rolls the ball into the empty net to put the hosts 1-0 up in double-quick time.

45 seconds

7 May 1955

United get off to an unbelievable start with one of the quickest FA Cup Final goals of all time. In front of a 100,000 Wembley crowd, Jackie Milburn wins a corner as his attempted cross is knocked out of play by Manchester City left-back Roy Little. Len White's corner finds Milburn on the corner of the six-yard box and his header hits the underside of the top left-hand crossbar giving the defender on the line and goalkeeper Bert Trautmann no chance. An incredible start to the game by 'Wor Jackie'.

57 seconds

15 January 2019

Sean Longstaff gets United off to a flyer in the FA Cup third-round replay away to Championship side Blackburn Rovers. A much-changed Newcastle had been held to a 1-1 draw at St James' Park, but took just 57 seconds to break the deadlock at Ewood Park, with Longstaff receiving a pass from Joselu outside the box before letting fly with a powerful drive from 20 yards that takes a huge deflection, wrong-foots the keeper and flies into the net. As the initial shot was on target, Longstaff is credited with the goal.

59 seconds

22 October 2016

Ayoze Perez scores the Magpies' fastest goal for 12 years to put United 1-0 up against Ipswich Town. In the Championship clash at St James' Park, Perez volleys home after a Dwight Gayle flick-on to put Newcastle on their way to a 3-0 victory and tenth win in 12 matches.

1

10 March 1993

Rob Lee gets table-topping United off to the perfect start against his old club Charlton Athletic. Chasing a long ball from defence, Lee gets behind the Addicks' defence – which has parted wide enough to drive a bus through the middle – and dispatches a powerful left-foot shot from just inside the box to get the Magpies off and running at St James' Park.

2

21 September 2002

Craig Bellamy gets the Magpies off to a dream start in the Tyne–Wear derby at St James' Park. With just 83 seconds on the clock, Bellamy grabs one of the quickest goals this fixture has ever seen after fine work between Alan Shearer and Kieron Dyer sets him clear to beat Thomas Sorensen and make it 1-0. The perfect opening and one that will put Sir Bobby Robson's side on the way to a much-needed three points against Sunderland.

3

4 February 1984

Newcastle's first visit to Fratton Park for 19 years starts perfectly as Chris Waddle breaks with pace from his own half, skipping past one challenge before playing the ball across to his right where Kevin Keegan receives the pass and then fires a low shot from 18 yards that just sneaks inside the near post to give the Magpies the lead against Portsmouth.

4 February 1989

Mirandinha anticipates a misplaced back pass and uses his pace to get onto the loose ball as it passes the keeper and tucks an angled shot into the empty net at a rain-lashed St James' Park. It is wonderful anticipation by the Brazilian who uses the wet conditions to his advantage, but it's still sloppy play by the Liverpool defence.

1 October 1991

It might not have been the most important competition, but the events at Prenton Park as United took on Tranmere Rovers in an extraordinary Zenith Data Systems Cup clash are worth documenting. The Magpies are soon ahead on The Wirral as Lee Clark's low drive hits Micky Quinn on its way and deflects into the top-left corner to make it 1-0 – but there will be another 11 goals to come in this absorbing contest.

16 April 1994

A memorable visit to Anfield gets the perfect start with just three minutes on the clock. Andy Cole plays a short pass to Rob Lee on the edge of the Liverpool box and the England midfielder neatly spins away from his marker before deftly lifting the ball over the onrushing David James for his sixth goal in eight games and to put Kevin Keegan's Magpies 1-0 up. Poignantly, it will be the last ever Newcastle United goal scored in front of Liverpool's iconic Kop terracing which is to be demolished a few weeks later, though not the outcome the masses of Liverpool fans on the famous old terrace had imagined.

21 August 1996

David Batty scores the best goal of his career (without doubt) to put United 1-0 up against Wimbledon. On a gloriously sunny day at St James' Park, a long ball is pumped towards the edge of the Wimbledon box – goalkeeper Neil Sullivan races out to head clear but his clearance only finds Batty who calmly chips the ball back over Sullivan and in off the underside of the crossbar to put Kevin Keegan's side ahead. Spare a thought for the Dons' keeper who had been beaten by a David Beckham shot from the halfway line the week before. For Batty, scoring was something of a rarity with just four goals in 114 appearances for United and a total of just nine in 558 career matches!

2 February 1997

Robbie Elliott gets Newcastle off and running with an early goal against Leicester City at St James' Park. Keith Gillespie beats the Leicester left-back before crossing into the middle where a scramble ensues. The ball comes out to Elliott just inside the box and his low, left-foot shot just has too much for the keeper, who can't keep the effort out.

25 January 1998

Alan Shearer gives the Magpies the lead in an FA Cup fourth-round tie away to Vauxhall Conference side Stevenage Borough. It's a game Newcastle are obviously expected to win – and win well – and when Shearer heads home Keith Gillespie's pinpoint cross early on, the non-League side must fear the worst. But Stevenage will level just before the break, hold on for a famous draw and earn a money-spinning replay at St James' Park.

4

21 November 1993

The start of what will be an extraordinary day against Liverpool for Andy Cole begins when Rob Lee is sent clear on the left wing and his inch-perfect cross is turned in at close range by Andy Cole for his 19th goal in just 17 appearances for the Magpies – a predatory strike by a natural goalscorer.

1 January 1997

Alan Shearer and Les Ferdinand combine again as Newcastle take an early lead against Leeds United at St James' Park. Coming on the back of a 7-1 win over Spurs just four days before, the Magpies roar into the New Year and continue where they left off as Ferdinand nods a corner back to the edge of the box for Shearer to volley a low shot home from 18 yards. It's the 24th goal the pair have managed in 19 games as a strike partnership. Lethal.

13 March 2005

Alan Shearer's hard work on the right flank sets up Patrick Kluivert to score the goal that takes United into the FA Cup semi-finals. Shearer's strength and pace sees him out-muscle Ledley King and the Magpies legend then powers into the box and plays the ball back to Kluivert to expertly finish with an angled shot from eight yards with only four minutes played. That will be enough to beat Spurs 1-0 at St James' Park and book a semi-final berth against Manchester United at Cardiff's Millennium Stadium.

7 November 2006

The Magpies take an early lead in the League Cup fifth-round tie away to Watford. With a place in the last eight awaiting the winners, Newcastle take the initiative when Emre's free kick is headed home by Antoine Sibierski from close range giving Hornets keeper Richard Lee no chance.

20 April 2008

United get off to the perfect start in the Tyne–Wear derby at St James' Park. Kevin Keegan's men went into the game unbeaten in five matches and with confidence high, and that shows in an opening that floors Sunderland. The creator is Geremi who sends in a superb cross that Michael Owen glances past Craig Gordon to send (most of) St James' Park wild.

5

31 August 1974

John Tudor puts Newcastle 1-0 up against West Ham United. On a murky afternoon at a packed St James' Park, Micky Burns carries the ball forward before lofting a pass towards Tudor on the left of the Hammers' box – though he mishits his shot as it lands, it bounces up and over the keeper to make it 1-0 for the Magpies.

15 August 1992

If Paul Bracewell's move from Sunderland to Newcastle had been controversial (they always are!), all doubts were forgotten just five minutes into his St James' Park debut. As Southend United struggled to clear their lines, the ball falls to Bracewell 25 yards out and the midfielder cracks a missile of a shot into the top-left corner of the net to make it 1-0 for Kevin Keegan's men – what a start for Bracewell, whose past associations are quickly put to one side.

9 May 1993

Second Division champions Newcastle set out to enjoy the final match of a wonderful season against Leicester City at a celebratory St James' Park. Kevin Keegan had brought the good times back to Tyneside with his brand of thrilling football and the Foxes were about to feel the full force of the Magpies' lethal strike force, lasting only five minutes before David Kelly receives a chipped pass in the box, then chests the ball down and fires it on target – the keeper does well to push it out but Andy Cole is on hand to prod the rebound home for his tenth goal in 12 games since joining the club.

16 January 1994

A chaotic mix-up in the Queens Park Rangers defence leads to Newcastle taking a 1-0 lead at Loftus Road. A short back pass by Clive Wilson sees Andy Cole race in on keeper Tony Roberts who saves at his feet, but the ball then pops out to Lee Clark on the edge of the box and his low angled drive finds the bottom-left corner of the net from 18 yards out to put the Magpies in front and give Clark his second goal of the campaign.

22 December 1999

United grab the early advantage over Tottenham in an FA Cup third-round replay at St James' Park. Having drawn 1-1 at White Hart Lane, the Magpies race out of the blocks and Warren Barton's cross from the right is headed down by Duncan Ferguson for Gary Speed to sweep home past keeper Ian Walker from close range.

15 September 2001

When Newcastle are awarded a free kick around 30 yards out against Manchester United, few believe Laurent Robert will have a strike at goal – but he does and the French winger's superb set piece flies over the wall, past Fabien Barthez and into the top-right corner to put the Magpies 1-0 at St James' Park against Sir Alex Ferguson's men.

19 February 2003

United take a vital early lead in the Champions League group stage tie away to Bayer Leverkusen. On what is Sir Bobby Robson's 70th birthday, Shola Ameobi strikes with barely five minutes played as Lomana LuaLua skips past Cris on the right before sending in a fine cross for Ameobi to nod home and make it 1-0 in Germany.

26 February 2003

Alan Shearer scores his first Champions League goal from open play in 14 attempts as he puts United 1-0 up against Bayer Leverkusen at St James' Park. The Magpies legend had missed the previous meeting a week earlier through injury but makes up for lost time with a typical predatory finish. Gary Speed sends in a teasing cross from the left and Shearer, pulling away from defender Diego Placente, meets the cross with a powerful diving header to finally break his duck at the ripe old age of 32.

6

14 May 1995

Ruel Fox scores his 12th goal of a fine campaign to put United 1-0 up at St James' Park against relegation-threatened Crystal Palace. Indeed, the visitors – knew that defeat would send them to the second tier, while a home victory could seal a UEFA Cup spot that had looked assured for most of the 1994/95 campaign. Fox carries the ball down the left flank, tormenting the Palace right-back before cutting inside of a couple of challenges and unleashing a right-foot shot from the edge of the box – the shot takes a huge deflection on its way into the back of the net and leaves the Palace keeper wrong-footed as Kevin Keegan's men look to end the season on a high.

14 May 2000

Great control and hold-up play by Alan Shearer ends with Gary Speed putting United 1-0 up against Arsenal at St James' Park. Shearer receives the ball inside the box and juggles it before clipping it over the head of Oleg Luzhny and into the path of Speed who volleys a low shot home from six yards out. Terrific innovation by the legendary No.9.

22 March 2007

United go 1-0 up as they bid to end a run of 14 games without victory in the Premier League. Of those games, Kevin Keegan, in his second spell as boss at St James' Park, has overseen ten games without a win so when Mark Viduka gets an early goal, the relief among the home fans is palpable. Viduka collects a pass from Geremi before firing a low drive past Fulham keeper Kasey Keller to raise hopes of a long-awaited victory on Tyneside.

29 October 2014

Rolando Aarons takes just six minutes to put the Magpies ahead against Manchester City at the Etihad Stadium in the League Cup. City, defending champions of the trophy, having beaten Sunderland at Wembley earlier in the year, are stunned when the 18-year-old Aarons intercepts a poor pass outside the box and then uses his pace to drift past Eliaquim Mangala before hitting a low angled shot through the legs of Willy Caballero to silence the home supporters.

7

10 September 1994

A thunderous opening goal sends St James' Park wild as Kevin Keegan's side grab an early lead against Chelsea. Andy Cole receives a pass just to the left of centre and drives into the Chelsea box and without a thought to do anything else unleashes a fierce left-foot shot that squeezes between the post and crossbar on its way into the roof of the net – a stunning strike from the red-hot Cole.

18 September 1994

The Magpies take an early lead away to Arsenal courtesy of a large slice of luck. As a cross into the Gunners' box is partially cleared, Peter Beardsley collects it some 30 yards out, drives forward and hits a low drive that takes a sizeable deflection off Martin Keown before beating David Seaman for the opening goal at Highbury.

3 May 1995

With three games remaining of the 1994/95 Premier League season, Newcastle's hopes of claiming a UEFA Cup spot hang in the balance with a tricky home game against Spurs at St James' Park. But the Magpies get off to a superb start and the opening goal is down to something of a role reversal with some great wing play by Steve Watson down the left and then a tempting cross into the six-yard box for Keith Gillespie to head powerfully home from close range to make it 1-0. Gillespie didn't score many headers so this is something of a collector's item.

24 April 2017

Needing a victory to secure promotion back to the Premier League, United get off to the perfect start against Preston North End at St James' Park. As a corner is whipped from the right, Ciaran Clark flicks on the ball at the near post and Ayoze Perez bundles the ball in at the far post to put the Magpies 1-0 up.

10 November 2018

Terrific work by DeAndre Yedlin sets up Salomon Rondon to score the first goal of the afternoon against Bournemouth. Having won their first game of the campaign just a week earlier against Watford, United are desperate to make it back-to-back wins and climb further clear of the relegation zone, and Yedlin's burst down the right ends with a low cross that Rondon initially fires as a shot straight at the keeper – but then tucks the rebound home to make it 1-0.

8

29 October 1983

Peter Beardsley sets Newcastle on their way to the 5-0 thrashing of Manchester City at St James' Park. City, also going well at the top of the Second Division, see their promotion ambitions take a serious blow against the imperious Magpies and Beardsley is at the heart of everything, jinking past a couple of challenges before scoring past City keeper Alex Williams from close range to make it 1-0. Beardsley will go on to complete his hat-trick with Kevin Keegan and Chris Waddle also on target in front of the 33,675 crowd.

17 December 1989

Struggling United get an early lead against Southampton. A long ball from defence is only half cleared by Ray Wallace and falls to Kevin Brock 25 yards out and his hopeful, bobbling shot somehow finds its way past Saints keeper Tim Flowers into the bottom-left corner to give the Magpies a 1-0 lead at St James' Park.

9

14 April 2004

Alan Shearer heads home to put United 1-0 up on the night and 2-1 up on aggregate in the UEFA Cup quarter-final second leg at St James' Park. Having held PSV Eindhoven 1-1 in the first leg, it is the perfect start for the Magpies as Shearer heads home at the near post from a Laurent Robert corner, connecting perfectly with the pacey cross to give the keeper no chance.

11 May 2009

United get an early leveller in the crucial relegation clash with Middlesbrough at St James' Park. Trailing from a third-minute own goal from Habib Beye, the Magpies fight back as Danny Guthrie's corner is headed home powerfully by Steven Taylor as the Toon battle for three points against north-east rivals.

12 May 2019

Matt Ritchie's low pass to the corner of the Fulham box finds Jonjo Shelvey in plenty of space and the United midfielder immediately hits a typically clean, sweet strike that flies like a missile into the top-left corner of the net to give the Magpies a 1-0 lead at Craven Cottage. Few United players can hit a ball as well as Shelvey.

10

26 December 1989

United score a first away goal in five games to draw level at Sheffield Wednesday. Trailing from an early David Hirst strike, the Magpies rally quickly and Kevin Brock's excellent free kick finds the head of former PSV Eindhoven star Rob McDonald at the far post and he makes no mistake from close range.

25 April 1993

In the first-ever live televised Tyne–Wear derby, Scott Sellars settles the game with only ten minutes on the clock. At a rain-sodden St James' Park, the Toon Army know that victory over Sunderland will edge United ever closer to a top-flight return with a chance to complete a league double for the first time in 36 years. When Newcastle are awarded a free kick on the edge of the box, a well-worked routine sees two players go to take it from different angles before Sellars steps up, lifts the ball over the wall and in off the left post to score the only goal of the match.

3 May 1995

United go 2-0 up against Spurs in a crucial Premier League clash at St James' Park. Already leading 1-0 from Keith Gillespie's header, the second is more conventional as Peter Beardsley's corner meets the head of Darren Peacock on the corner of the six-yard box and he glances the ball past keeper Ian Walker and into the far left of the Tottenham net for his first goal for the club since joining from QPR the previous summer.

3 April 1996

Brilliant work by Faustino Asprilla brings the Magpies level away to Liverpool. The move begins on the right of the box where Asprilla nutmegs a defender, moves into the box and then pulls the ball back for Les Ferdinand, who swivels and sends a powerful shot high into the roof of the net to make it 1-1.

11

23 December 1995

Terrific trickery by David Ginola creates a chance out of nothing that ends with United taking the lead against Nottingham Forest. The French winger performs a Cruyff Turn to lose one defender, then draws in another two Forest players towards him before nudging the ball to his right for Rob Lee to unleash a howitzer of a shot into the top-right corner from fully 30 yards out – a wonderful goal and it puts Kevin Keegan's men 1-0 up.

19 September 1999

In a game between the Premier League's two most out-of-sorts teams, United host Sheffield Wednesday at St James' Park in what is Sir Bobby Robson's first home game in charge since taking over. In desperate need of a lift, the Magpies get off to the perfect start when Aaron Hughes heads home Kieron Dyer's teasing cross from the left, rising higher than his marker to nod down and past the keeper from eight yards out to send a delighted home crowd wild.

5 February 2000

The Magpies take an early lead in their first-ever visit to Sunderland's Stadium of Light. It's a fortuitous goal, too – though nobody in black and white is complaining

– as Didier Domi receives the ball just inside the Black Cats' box and hits a low drive that takes a wicked deflection as it goes past the wrong-footed goalkeeper to send 3,000 United fans wild at the opposite end of the ground.

26 February 2003

United go 2-0 up in quick-fire time against a Bayer Leverkusen side who had reached the previous season's Champions League Final. Alan Shearer scored the opening goal on five minutes and this time he starts and finishes the move that puts the Magpies firmly in command. Leverkusen defender Cris – who had cost his side two goals in the group stage clash in Germany – was again badly at fault as he played a lazy pass across the back four that Shearer intercepts and plays in Shola Ameobi who jinks his way into the box and to the touchline before sending a low cross that both keeper Hans-Jorg Butt and Cris (again!) combined fail to clear, and the ball bobbles to Shearer at the far post to gently head home. He'd waited many years for his first Champions League goal from open play and now he had scored two in six minutes!

11 August 2007

Charles N'Zogbia gets United's season off and running away to Bolton Wanderers. In what is Sam Allardyce's first game in charge of the Magpies – against the club where he made his name in management – N'Zogbia shapes up to take a free kick on the right of the Bolton box. He sends in a low, left-foot cross with curl into the six-yard box and by the time keeper Jussi Jaaskelainen realises no Newcastle player is going to connect with the cross, it is already too late and the ball skips off the turf and into the bottom-left corner of the net to make it 1-0 for the visitors.

12 May 2019

The Magpies' flying start away to Fulham gets even better with a second goal in two minutes at Craven Cottage. Matt Ritchie – who assisted the opening goal – plays Christian Atsu in on the left of the Fulham box and he cuts in and fires a weak shot at keeper Sergio Rico who makes a hash of the save and Ayoze Perez slides in to tap the loose ball home from two yards out.

12

17 March 1984

Having fallen behind to a Middlesbrough goal after just three minutes, United quickly draw level at St James' Park. There seems little danger as Peter Beardsley plays a short pass to Kevin Keegan who manages to hold off a challenge from behind and loop a return pass to Beardsley, who motors towards the box before spotting the keeper slightly off his line and then curling a measured shot into the far-right corner of the net.

18 October 1992

Chasing numerous club and national records, Kevin Keegan's expansive Second Division leaders travelled the short distance down the A1 to take on Sunderland at Roker Park – a venue the Magpies hadn't won at for some 36 years. A 12th successive victory would equal Tottenham's double-winning side of the 1960s and also match the best unbeaten Newcastle start since 1950, so there was plenty at stake in this particular Tyne–Wear derby. And it was Keegan's 100 per cent side who struck first. Rob Lee gets in behind the Black Cats' defence before playing a square ball across the six-yard box that Sunderland's Gary Owers slides past his own keeper to make it 1-0 to the visitors.

12 March 1994

Peter Beardsley scores the opening goal on what will be a record-equalling day for the Magpies at St James' Park. After a spot kick is awarded against struggling Swindon Town, Beardsley tucks his penalty to the left of the keeper, who manages to get a hand on it but can't prevent it crossing the line to put Kevin Keegan's Europe-chasing side 1-0 up.

20 October 1996

The Magpies take an early lead in the title clash with Manchester United at St James' Park – though under controversial circumstances. A corner from the left finds the head of Alan Shearer who nods it back across the six-yard box and Darren Peacock heads towards goal but his effort lacks power. The ball still finds its way past Peter Schmeichel, and Dennis Irwin makes a desperate attempt to clear the ball off the line – TV replays suggest he probably just managed to stop all of the ball crossing the line but the assistant referee flags for a goal and the referee agrees. The Manchester United players protest long and hard but – long before goal-line technology would have cleared the matter up for certain – the official is having none of it and waves the Manchester United players away. The Magpies celebrate accordingly.

22 August 2011

After John Carew misses an early penalty for Aston Villa, Joey Barton gives United the lead shortly after in the opening St James' Park fixture of the 2011/12 campaign. Jonas Gutierrez plays a short pass to Barton on the edge of the Villa box and the former Manchester City midfielder tees himself up before firing a thunderous drive past the keeper from 20 yards out.

5 November 2011

United continue their superb start to the 2011/12 season against Everton at St James' Park. Having remained unbeaten in their opening ten Premier League matches, Alan Pardew's side look to continue their momentum against the Toffees and are handed an early bonus when Danny Simpson's inviting cross from the right is turned into his own net by Johnny Heitinga with Leon Best waiting to turn the ball home had the Everton defender missed it.

13 September 2016

On what will be a memorable night in West London, United take the lead against Queens Park Rangers at Loftus Road. Aleksandar Mitrovic bursts down the right flank before pulling a cross back to the edge of the Rangers box – Jonjo Shelvey hits a meaty shot but it takes a couple of deflections, wrong-footing the keeper completely before trickling over the line to give Rafa Benitez's side the advantage.

13

9 May 1993

The superb Rob Lee scores his 13th of a memorable campaign as he puts United 2-0 up against Leicester City at St James' Park. It's a goal out of nothing, too, as Lee receives a throw-in on the right before playing a short pass to Andy Cole in the box. Cole nudges a pass back to Lee who takes a touch before sending a rising right-foot shot past the keeper and into the far corner of the net from a tight angle to double the champions' advantage.

10 November 2013

Loic Remy scores what will be the only goal of the game at White Hart Lane as United record a hard-fought 1-0 win over Spurs. Yoan Gouffran chases down Spurs defender Paulinho before threading a pass through to Remy who rounds keeper Brad Friedel before rolling the ball into the empty net. Spurs will force Tim Krull into 14 saves and have 31 shots but the Magpies cling on and still travel home with a clean sheet and three points.

14

3 April 1996

Having equalised just four minutes earlier, Les Ferdinand provides the assist for United to take a 2-1 lead in a breathtaking start to the game at Anfield. From just inside his own half, the England forward plays a ball to the left and into the path of David Ginola, who had got behind the Liverpool defence – the French playmaker carries the ball until just inside the box where he fires a low left-foot shot past the keeper to stun the Kop (again).

15

11 May 1968

The Magpies are involved in a thrilling end to the 1967/68 season as they host Manchester City on the final day of the campaign. If City win, they are Division One champions, while Manchester United host Sunderland knowing if City lose and they win, the title will instead be heading back to Old Trafford. At St James' Park and with perhaps 15,000 travelling fans dotted around the ground, the Blues had taken an early lead on 13 minutes, but Newcastle hit back within 90 seconds as Bryan Robson's angled run into the City box from the right sees him hit a powerful shot across keeper Ken Mulhearn and into the bottom-left corner to make it 1-1.

21 November 1993

Newcastle go 2-0 up with only 15 minutes played and Andy Cole scores his second of the match in a blistering start by the Magpies at St James' Park. Peter Beardsley receives the ball midway inside the Liverpool half and he draws four players around him before slipping a pass out to Scott Sellars on the left wing. Sellars moves towards the box before playing a low cross to exactly where Cole is pointing and the Newcastle No.9 makes no mistake from six yards to score his 20th goal of the campaign.

19 February 2003

Out-of-sorts Bayer Leverkusen defender Cris fails to clear a through ball and only gifts possession to Shola Ameobi who skips past Kleine before firing a superb left-foot shot past Hans-Jorg Butt to score his second of the game as the Magpies get off to a blistering start in the Champions League group stage tie in Germany.

5 December 2019

Newcastle go 1-0 up away to Premier League surprise package Sheffield United. Javier Manquillo receives the ball just to the right of the Blades' box and his cross into the middle finds the head of Allan Saint-Maximin who manages to direct the ball just out of Dean Henderson's reach to the delight of the travelling United fans at Bramall Lane to make it 1-0.

4 February 2020

United grab an early advantage away to League One side Oxford United in the FA Cup fourth-round tie at the Kassam Stadium. The opener comes when the ball is played to Sean Longstaff on the edge of the Oxford box – he bides his time and, despite being faced with six Oxford players, none of them press the Newcastle man and he nudges it right before curling a right-foot shot into the top-right corner to make it 1-0 for the Magpies.

16

4 February 1998

Alan Shearer settles the St James' Park nerves with a goal on 16 minutes against non-League side Stevenage Borough. In the FA Cup fourth-round replay, Shearer heads Alessandro Pistone's cross down and past the keeper and, despite a spectacular overhead clearance by a defender, the eagle-eyed linesman spotted the ball had crossed the line – just – and the goal is awarded.

17

2 October 1999

Alan Shearer bags his ninth goal in four games for United as he heads home against Middlesbrough. The Magpies No.9 benefits from a great run and cross in from the right by Warren Barton and though the Boro defender seems to have the edge as the ball comes in,, Shearer muscles his way ahead to nod past the keeper and put Newcastle 1-0 up.

29 December 2002

After an entertaining opening in which both teams had chances to score, it is Newcastle who break the deadlock against Tottenham with 17 minutes on the clock. The goal comes as a result of a long Laurent Robert throw-in that Spurs defender Goran Bunjevcevic clears only as far as Gary Speed who drills a crisp shot home from 12 yards to put Sir Bobby Robson's high-flying side 1-0 up.

18

12 March 1994

Rob Lee races in behind the Swindon Town defence as he chases a long pass from inside the Newcastle half and, as he is about to be challenged on the edge of the box, he unleashes a powerful rising shot into the top-right corner of the net to put the Magpies 2-0 up against the rocking Robins.

29 April 1996

After seeing a 12-point lead over Manchester United evaporate in the second half of the campaign, the Magpies travel to Elland Road looking for the three points that will keep their Premier League title hopes alive. In a tense affair, the travelling United fans don't have to wait too long for what will prove to be the only goal of the game as Peter Beardsley's corner is nodded back across by Les Ferdinand and Keith Gillespie guides (another) rare headed goal past keeper Mark Beeney to secure three vital points. Afterwards, boss Kevin Keegan shows the pressure is taking its toll as he delivers his famous 'Love it, love it' rant aimed at Manchester United boss Sir Alex Ferguson and his manipulation and obvious mind games in the previous days and weeks.

12 May 2013

United level the scores in the crucial relegation scrap with Queens Park Rangers at Loftus Road. Having fallen behind to a Loic Remy penalty on 11 minutes, just seven minutes later the Magpies are awarded a spot kick of their own after Jose Bosingwa pulls Hatem Ben Arfa's shirt in the box. Ben Arfa himself steps up to thump the ball in off the underside of the crossbar and makes it 1-1 – it's his first goal for six months.

19

18 February 1984

Having beaten Second Division promotion rivals Manchester City 5-0 at St James' Park earlier in the season, the Magpies travelled to Maine Road expecting a stiffer examination from the Blues, but United – backed by more than 6,000 travelling fans in the 41,767 crowd, the biggest Newcastle had played in front of that campaign – strike first when Chris Waddle's cross into the box from the right is flicked on by Kevin Keegan and Peter Beardsley skips a challenge before drilling the ball past keeper Alex Williams to make it 1-0.

2 May 2012

The Magpies' hopes of Champions League football increase dramatically with a superb away win at top-four rivals Chelsea. The opening goal is a sumptuous strike from Papiss Cisse as he receives a short pass from Davide Santon on the edge of the box and then flicks the ball up with his right foot and lashes a left-foot volley past Petr Cech for his 12th goal in 12 games for United.

20

4 January 1994

A proud moment for Peter Beardsley who scores his 200th career goal to put the Magpies on level terms against Norwich City at Carrow Road. With Newcastle trailing to an early strike from the home side, Beardsley moves in from the right flank, plays a one-two with Lee Clark which he just about manages to squeeze through a couple of challenges before tucking a low shot past Bryan Gunn from close range.

28 December 1996

Newcastle take the lead against Spurs at St James' Park with a thumping effort from Alan Shearer. As a long pass from the back is flicked on by Les Ferdinand, there is still plenty for Shearer to do, but he gets to the ball first, knocks it over a defender's challenge on the edge of the box before chesting it down and then volleying a shot into the top-right corner of the net to make it 1-0. A superb Shearer goal.

19 April 2010

Needing just a point to be crowned Championship champions, United take the lead at Home Park against Plymouth Argyle. The opening goal comes when a corner is floated to the edge of the six-yard box and

Andy Carroll leaps to head the ball with precision into the top right-hand corner of the net – his 18th of the season – and sends thousands of travelling fans into raptures at the opposite end of the stadium.

21

18 February 1984

Newcastle go 2-0 up at Second Division promotion contenders Manchester City. Kenny Wharton's free kick from the left is cleared but City striker Derek Parlane gifts possession back to Terry McDermott who plays an incisive ball with the outside of his boot to Kevin Keegan, who hits a first-time shot from just inside the box past Alex Williams to double the Magpies' advantage on the way to a priceless 2-1 win at Maine Road.

3 September 1993

An odd sight for the Toon Army watching United come out wearing their away colours of electric blue to host Sheffield Wednesday. Both sides wore striped shirts for home matches and the Owls' away strip also clashed with the Newcastle home kit so the officials demanded a change. It wouldn't affect proceedings, however, with the Magpies taking the lead when Malcolm Allen's low shot was pushed out by the keeper and Andy Cole, following up, tucks the ball into the bottom corner from 12 yards to make it 1-0.

8 January 1994

The Magpies take the lead in the FA Cup third-round tie against Coventry City. Having survived a couple of early scares, Peter Beardsley is inevitably at the heart of the move that breaks the deadlock as he cleverly exchanges passes with Scott Sellars and it is Beardsley's low angled shot that cannons back off the far post and straight into the path of Andy Cole who immediately prods the loose ball into the empty net, much to the delight of the majority of the 35,444 crowd.

10 September 1994

Ruel Fox is fastest to react as Rob Lee's penalty is saved by Dmitri Kharine. Lee's low effort is pushed away by the Chelsea keeper but Fox races in to put a low shot into the back of the net from a few yards out to put the Magpies 2-1 up at St James' Park. Kharine, understandably, is not best pleased with his slow-reacting defenders.

5 February 2000

It's a dream start to the Tyne–Wear derby at Sunderland's new home, the Stadium of Light. Already leading through Didier Domi's deflected effort, the Magpies keep the pressure up on the home defence with a series of crosses into the box – though the danger is scrambled clear, Kieron Dyer again attempts to fire a cross in from the left before being fouled. Dyer takes the free kick and Helder rises to head home from close range to make it 2-0, though Sunderland eventually fight back to earn a 2-2 draw.

11 August 2007

A spectacular effort from Obafemi Martins puts United 2-0 up away to Bolton Wanderers in Sam Allardyce's first game in charge of the Magpies. There seems no particular threat as James Milner looks into the box from the left wing, but his cross finds Martins who chests the ball down and then acrobatically sends an overhead kick past Jussi Jaaskelainen to double the lead with only 21 minutes on the clock.

22

12 May 1984

Kevin Keegan scores his final goal for Newcastle United at an emotional St James' Park. The Magpies, already assured of promotion back to the First Division along with Sheffield Wednesday and Chelsea, were in celebratory mood, with many of the 36,286 crowd coming to say goodbye to Keegan, who had announced he would retire after the game. Just as he had marked his debut with a goal, Keegan scores on his farewell appearance, reacting quickest after Chris Waddle's low drive strikes the foot of the post to tap into an empty net. It is Keegan's 49th goal in just 85 appearances as he brings a magnificent career to a close.

18 August 1993

The name of Peter Atherton may not be that well known among the Toon Army, but the Coventry City defender owns a curious piece of Magpies history. Atherton's outstretched foot as a low United free kick came into the Sky Blues' box was enough to divert the ball past his own keeper and give Newcastle a 1-0 lead at Highfield Road – it was also newly promoted United's first-ever Premiership (as was the name back then) goal.

28 December 1996

The Magpies strike for a second time in little more than two minutes to go 2-0 up against Spurs. Kevin Keegan's side turn up the heat after Alan Shearer's opener and it pays dividends as Keith Gillespie's cross is only cleared as far as Peter Beardsley who takes a slight touch, fires in a low shot and Les Ferdinand toe-pokes home from close range to put United firmly in control at St James' Park.

17 September 1997

Faustino Asprilla keeps his cool to put Newcastle 1-0 up against Barcelona in the Champions League Group C clash at St James' Park. It is just reward for the fiery Colombian after he chased a Jon Dahl Tomasson ball into the box only to be brought down by the keeper as he attempted to go around him. The referee awards a penalty and, after what seems like an age, Asprilla tucks the ball just out of the keeper's reach to send the United fans wild.

15 January 2019

A goal made by youth and scored by youth as Rafa Benitez's much-changed Newcastle side go 2-0 up in the FA Cup third-round replay with Blackburn Rovers. Jacob Murphy gets into the box and sees his shot saved by the keeper, but he collects the rebound on the right, then beats the full-back before whipping a low centre for Callum Roberts to volley home from six yards to double the Magpies' advantage. It is Roberts's first goal for United.

23

14 May 2000

Alan Shearer powers home his 300th career goal as he restores the Magpies' lead against Arsenal. With United seeing their early lead wiped out immediately by Nwankwo Kanu, a free kick on the edge of the Gunners' box gives Shearer an opportunity from 20 yards. He runs up and blasts a shot past the wall and into the top-left corner of the net to make it 2-1 and record his 30th goal of the campaign, his 199th league goal and his landmark 300th career goal.

20 November 2001

Dwight Gayle punishes a glaring error by Leeds United keeper Rob Green to put United ahead at Elland Road. Jack Colback's clever cross-cum-shot from 40 yards on the left flank sees Green push the ball out instead of catching it and, from a yard or so out, Gayle is in there like a flash to poke home to make it 1-0 for Rafa Benitez's side.

7 May 2017

A lovely flowing move ends with United taking the lead against Barnsley at St James' Park. With Newcastle trailing leaders Brighton & Hove Albion by two points on the final day of the 2016/17 Championship season,

DeAndre Yedlin runs on to a clever pass and crosses low from the right to Ayoze Perez, who superbly back-flicks the ball past the keeper from the corner of the six-yard box to make it 1-0.

13 May 2018

On the final day of the campaign, the Magpies save arguably their best display of the season to dismantle Antonio Conte's Chelsea at St James' Park. The opening goal finally arrives – after a host of near misses and fine saves – when Matt Ritchie's cross finds Jacob Murphy and his effort bounces up on to the bar and then falls into the path of Dwight Gayle who taps in from a yard out.

24

1 October 1991

Micky Quinn grabs his second of the night to make it 2-2 away to Tranmere Rovers in the Zenith Data Systems Cup at Prenton Park. Gavin Peacock's low cross sees a shot fired in, the keeper spills the ball and Quinn is on hand to prod home from a couple of yards out.

11 December 2002

Shola Ameobi – playing because of injuries to Alan Shearer and Craig Bellamy – stuns the Nou Camp as he brings United level in the Champions League group stage clash with Barcelona. Having fallen behind the Catalan side on seven minutes, the Magpies equalise with only their second attack of the game as Nolberto Solano slips the ball to Kieron Dyer on the edge of the box and he in turn finds the unmarked Ameobi who slots the ball past Bonano.

28 September 2016

Matt Ritchie's clever cross with the outside of his boot finds Dwight Gayle on the edge of the six-yard box to put United 1-0 up against Norwich City at St James' Park in what will be a thrilling Championship encounter. The Canaries are looking to go top of the table, while the Magpies know defeat could leave them as low as tenth.

25

31 August 1974

Having set the first goal up for John Tudor, Micky Burns claims his second assist of the afternoon against West Ham United as he skips past the left-back with ease before sending a deep cross from the right flank towards the back post for Malcolm Macdonald to head home powerfully and make it 2-0 for the Magpies and, with no further goals in the game, secure victory for the hosts, who had also seen Terry McDermott miss a penalty between the two strikes.

23 December 1995

United regain the lead after being pegged back by Nottingham Forest at St James' Park. It is once again David Ginola – in irresistible form – who does the damage, receiving the ball inside the Forest half before drawing no less than five players towards him – but none close him down and he elects to shoot from 20 yards out with his low shot beating keeper Mark Crossley and nestling in the bottom right of the net to make it 2-1 at St James' Park.

21 December 2013

Yohan Cabaye opens the scoring as the Magpies look for a sixth win in eight games and also record a fourth straight away win in the Premier League. Alan Pardew returns to his old Crystal Palace stomping ground as United look to stay in touch with the top four. The influential Cabaye tucks away a shot from ten yards that takes a slight deflection off Mile Jedinak to give Pardew's men a 1-0 lead at windswept Selhurst Park.

30 November 2019

United take just three minutes to level the score against Manchester City at St James' Park. Though the visitors had largely dominated and gone ahead through Raheem Sterling, Miguel Almiron progresses into the City box before squaring a pass to full-back Jetro Willems who lets the ball come across his body before firing an angled shot into the bottom-right corner of the net to make it 1-1 against the Premier League champions.

26

21 August 1971

Malcolm Macdonald scores his first Newcastle United goal in a home clash with Liverpool. Trailing 1-0 to Emlyn Hughes's goal, John Tudor finds David Young's run into the box and as he skips past Keegan, the Liverpool forward brings him crashing to the turf. Supermac steps up to take the spot kick and emphatically plants the ball into the top-left corner, giving Ray Clemence no chance and levelling the scores in the process.

14 May 1995

Ruel Fox continues to be the scourge of the Crystal Palace defence as he sets up United's second goal of the game. The skilful winger takes – and beats – the Palace right-back before sending a cross into the six-yard box where Rob Lee arrives at the optimum moment to put Newcastle 2-0 up at St James' Park.

12 February 2000

Duncan Ferguson puts the Magpies a goal up against Manchester United. It's a superb strike from the big Scot as Alan Shearer expertly glances a long ball in to his strike partner on the edge of the United box. Ferguson, with his back to goal, allows the ball to move past him before turning and lashing a left-foot howitzer of a shot into the top-right corner of the net, giving Mark Bosnich no chance. A stunning goal from the big Scot.

31 October 2010

United make the breakthrough in the Tyne–Wear derby with a spectacular opening goal. A corner into the Sunderland box sees Mike Williamson and two Sunderland defenders compete for the header and the ball bounces down into the six-yard box where Kevin Nolan, back to goal, sends a powerful overhead kick into the roof of the net to make it 1-0 in what will be a Halloween horror for the Black Cats.

27

22 December 1999

Newcastle expose Spurs' weakness in the air to take a 2-0 lead in the FA Cup third-round replay. Nolberto Solano's corner finds the head of Nikos Dabizas and he makes no mistake with a firm header across the keeper and into the left corner of the net.

11 August 2007

As brilliant as Obafemi Martins's first goal against Bolton Wanderers had been, his second was somewhat fortuitous to say the least. Leading 2-0 already, Newcastle attack the home defence yet again and when Martins tries a hopeful shot from 20 yards or so out, it looks no more than a pass back to the Bolton keeper. But the shot takes the merest of deflections from Jlloyd Samuel to ever so slightly wrong-foot Jussi Jaaskelainen and roll gently past him into the net to give United a 3-0 opening-day lead at the Reebok and continue a remarkable start for former Bolton legend Sam Allardyce in his first game in charge of the Magpies.

22 September 2010

Newcastle draw level with Chelsea at Stamford Bridge in round three of the League Cup. With United having fallen behind to an early goal, Shane Ferguson's tempting cross is turned in past keeper Ross Turnbull by Nile Ranger at close range to make it 1-1 on the night.

25 August 2019

On a day of firsts, United record an impressive victory against Spurs at the newly completed Tottenham Hotspur Stadium. It is the Magpies' first visit to the North London side's sparkling new home and more than 3,000 jubilant travelling fans head back north after witnessing Joelinton's long-awaited first goal for the club. Christian Atsu spots the Brazilian's run in behind the Spurs defence and chips a ball into his path – he takes one touch to control and then fires into the bottom-left corner to score what will be the only goal of the game. It is also manager Steve Bruce's first victory since taking over at St James' Park.

28

1 October 1988

Trailing 1-0 after just three minutes and without a win at Anfield for 38 years, the Toon Army must have expected to head back to the north-east empty-handed yet again – but John Hendrie had other ideas as he chases a superb left flank pass from Michael O'Neill into the Liverpool box before drilling a low shot that goes through the keeper to make it 1-1.

9 May 1993

United continue to run riot against Leicester City, going 3-0 up with less than half an hour played on what will be a long afternoon for the visitors. Top scorer David Kelly, playing his 57th match of the season in all competitions, heads home from Lee Clark's cross into the box to score his 25th of the season and effectively seal the points with more than an hour of the final match of the campaign still remaining.

1 January 1994

United take a 1-0 lead against a struggling Manchester City at St James' Park. Scott Sellars wins possession on the right flank before moving forward and crossing into the box for Peter Beardsley to head back across to the unmarked Andy Cole who nods home from five yards out to continue his red-hot streak for United.

14 May 1995

The Magpies boost their chances of claiming a UEFA Cup berth as they continue to mercilessly tear FA Cup finalists Crystal Palace to shreds at a capacity St James' Park. The third goal comes when Keith Gillespie is allowed to run at the Palace defence unchallenged before unleashing a rising shot from 20 yards that gives the keeper no chance. That makes it 3-0, and though Palace rally after the break and pull a couple back through Chris Armstrong and Ray Houghton, Keegan's men hold on for a 3-2 victory. The result relegates Palace and saves the skin of Aston Villa, but doesn't get the Magpies into Europe with a sixth-place Premier League finish not enough and Leeds United and Liverpool instead qualify for the UEFA Cup – a harsh end for what had been such a promising start to the season.

19 April 2010

Superb play by Joey Barton sees United double the lead away to Plymouth. With Newcastle needing a point to be confirmed as Championship champions, Barton spins away from a challenge just inside his own half before nutmegging another Plymouth player and playing a quick one-two with a team-mate. Then, the former Manchester City man plays a precision ball into the path of Wayne Routledge on the right and he nicks it around the advancing keeper before hitting a low angled shot just inside the near post and making it 2-0 for United. There will be no further scoring and the Magpies win the second-tier title but hosts Plymouth Argyle are relegated to League One as a result of the loss.

29

22 July 2006

Shola Ameobi puts United ahead for the first time in the Intertoto Cup second leg with Lillestrom. Having been held by the Norwegians at St James' Park, the first goal in the return was always going to be crucial and Ameobi – bidding to fill the sizeable boots vacated by Alan Shearer – opens the scoring when he is first to react as Charles N'Zogbia's free kick is parried by Fredriksen and after skipping around a defender, Ameobi coolly slots home to put the Magpies 1-0 up.

5 November 2011

The Magpies go 2-0 up against Everton with less than half an hour played. It's a spectacular second too, with – almost inevitably – Ryan Taylor the scorer. Jack Rodwell heads a long throw clear, but only to Taylor 25 yards from goal and the talented United defender chests the ball down before volleying a ferocious drive that beats Tim Howard, crashes off the underside of the bar and bounces down and into the net to effectively seal what will be a 2-1 victory for Alan Pardew's unbeaten side. It is the first time since the 1994/95 season that United have remained unbeaten in their opening 11 matches.

30

21 November 1993

Andy Cole completes a glorious 26-minute hat-trick as he bags what will be the final goal of a 3-0 win over Liverpool at St James' Park. What is Cole's 21st goal of the season comes when a short pass is played into the feet of Rob Lee who immediately slices the Liverpool defence open with a sublime pass to Scott Sellars and his low cross is turned in by Cole at close range. For the Merseysiders it's a little like Groundhog Day with all three goals the results of low crosses into the box from the left and finished at close range by Cole.

20 October 1996

A superb goal puts Newcastle further ahead in the battle of the Uniteds at St James' Park. There seems little threat when Warren Barton plays a short pass to the feet of David Ginola on the left corner of the Manchester United box. But the French winger first holds off a challenge and then tees himself up, spins around and unleashes a ferocious shot into the top-right corner of Peter Schmeichel's net to send the home fans wild and put the Magpies 2-0 up.

17 September 1997

United take a 2-0 lead over Barcelona in the Champions League. It's a goal made in England, but created by a Northern Irishman and scored by a Colombian as Keith Gillespie takes on the left-back, beats him and whips in a terrific cross into the six-yard box where Faustino Asprilla arrives on cue to leap high and thump an unstoppable header past the goalkeeper to double Newcastle's lead against the Catalan giants and put St James' Park into dreamland.

19 September 1999

A deft volley is the start of a record five-goal haul for Alan Shearer against Sheffield Wednesday. On an afternoon that will showcase the very best of the Magpies legend's full gamut of finishing techniques, he makes it 2-0 on the day as he expertly guides a Nolberto Solano cross from the left past the keeper from ten yards with a superb low volley.

13 September 2016

The Magpies go 2-0 up with only a half hour played at Loftus Road, with Matt Ritchie the creator. The former Bournemouth midfielder sends a precise low cross from midway inside the QPR half on the left, and the ball finds its way to Ayoze Perez who controls it and then fires a low angled drive in – the shot is saved, but the ball comes back to Perez who calmly rolls a shot back past the keeper and just inside the far post to double United's lead.

4 February 2020

Having scored the opening goal, Sean Longstaff then assists the second as the Magpies take a 2-0 lead in the fourth-round FA Cup tie away to Oxford United. Longstaff picks up possession just outside his own box and then sends a 60-yard pass into the path of Joelinton who controls the ball, moves into the Oxford box and then clips a shot past the keeper to put United firmly in control against the League One side.

31

24 April 1974

In front of a capacity St James' Park crowd, United level the score against Burnley in the 1974 Texaco Cup Final. Having seen off Birmingham City and Dundee United to get to the final, the Toon Army were keen to see Gordon Lee's side lift some silverware – no matter what it was – but Paul Fletcher had given the Clarets a 25th-minute lead. Within six minutes, the Magpies were level with Malcolm Macdonald the scorer and, with no further goals in normal time, extra time needed to be played. Fast forward to 103 minutes to find out what happened!

26 October 1988

Newcastle get an unexpected bonus as they take a 1-0 lead against Middlesbrough at St James' Park. With passions and emotion high following the recent passing of United legend Jackie Milburn, the home crowd urge the basement Magpies on and, as a cross comes into the box, it is Boro defender Gary Pallister who guides a header past his own keeper and into the bottom-left corner of the net.

21 October 1995

Keith Gillespie's excellent cross picks out Steve Howey who loops his header past Wimbledon keeper Paul

Heald and into the far left of the goal to give the Magpies a 1-0 lead against injury-hit Wimbledon. It will be the start of a long and miserable afternoon for the Wombles against Kevin Keegan's rampant high-flying side.

22 August 2011

United double their lead in the St James' Park sunshine as Jose Enrique raids down the left flank before sending a deep cross towards the back post. Andy Carroll leaps to head it back to the edge of the six-yard box where Kevin Nolan then heads towards goal – his effort is pushed back out by the Aston Villa keeper, but only back towards Nolan who thumps a diving header home to make it 2-0.

32

19 February 2003

Having just conceded to hosts Bayer Leverkusen in the Champions League group stage tie, the Magpies restore their two-goal first-half advantage as the otherwise impressive Oliver Neuville is dispossessed on the touchline by Laurent Robert whose cross from the left is met with an emphatic first-time volley by Lomana LuaLua to make it 3-1 on the night.

22 September 2010

A second goal in five minutes puts the Magpies 2-1 up at Stamford Bridge against a Chelsea side unbeaten in all competitions. Ryan Taylor adds to his selection of set-piece specials when he fires a powerful free kick – awarded for a foul on Shola Ameobi – around the wall and into the top corner of the net from 20 yards to make it 2-1.

33

19 September 1999

United race into a 3-0 lead at St James' Park against Sheffield Wednesday as Alan Shearer scores his second of the afternoon. The goal comes as a result of Shearer's industry on the right, and his deflected low cross is met by Warren Barton who sees his attempt strike the raised arm of Emerson Thome. The resulting penalty is struck home by Shearer who is, by then, well on his way to an unforgettable afternoon.

4 January 2012

Demba Ba puts a spanner in the works of Manchester United's title challenge on what will be a memorable evening at St James' Park for the Magpies and the perfect start to the New Year for Alan Pardew's talented side. A long ball towards the Reds' box is flicked on by Shola Ameobi and as it lands at the feet of Ba, he spins around and hits a clever rising shot from ten yards that loops over David de Gea and into the left corner of the net to send the Magpies' fans wild.

3 March 2020

Allan Saint-Maximin at his blistering best creates the opening goal of the FA Cup fifth-round tie away to West Bromwich Albion. Saint-Maximin wriggles away from a couple of challenges on the left flank before cutting into the Albion half and playing a precise through pass to Miguel Almiron who tucks a low left-foot shot past the onrushing keeper to put the Magpies 1-0 up at The Hawthorns.

34

9 May 1993

David Kelly rattles in goal number 26 of the season – his second in six minutes – as the Magpies show why they are deserved champions of the second tier. Like his first goal, Kelly has Lee Clark to thank as the midfielder gets into the Foxes' box on the left before playing a short pass for Kelly to sweep home in front of an ecstatic St James' Park crowd and make the scoreline 4-0.

19 March 1994

Rob Lee, a boyhood West Ham United fan, opens the scoring at Upton Park with a goal that is somewhat fortuitous. Lee spins around his marker before playing a pass into the feet of Andy Cole who tees up Lee to hit a shot from the edge of the box that takes a huge deflection off a defender on its way into the opposite side of the net the keeper was guarding.

15 September 2001

A goalkeeping howler from Fabien Barthez puts Newcastle back in front against Manchester United at St James' Park. Rob Lee collects the ball midway into the Reds' half and is allowed to progress to within 25 yards where he decides to take a punt from distance. Lee's low but powerful effort seems to go through

Barthez and flies up into the back of the net to make it 2-1 at St James' Park.

1 January 2007

A stunning James Milner goal puts Newcastle 1-0 up against Manchester United at St James' Park. The visitors, with a nine-point advantage at the top of the Premier League, can do nothing about Milner's strike as he cuts inside from the left flank before firing an unstoppable rising shot past Edwin van der Sar to give the Magpies a surprise lead.

31 October 2010

Kevin Nolan gets his second of the afternoon as United go 2-0 up against Sunderland in the latest Tyne–Wear derby tussle. There is a large slice of luck involved as Jonas Gutierrez fires a low shot that is partially blocked and lands at the feet of Andy Carroll who wrestles for possession and the ball then finds its way across to Nolan who rolls a shot past the keeper from close range to send St James' Park wild.

22 August 2011

In a memorable first home game of the season, the Magpies go 3-0 up against Aston Villa. It's a somewhat scrappy affair, as a corner is headed down by Mike Williamson and it eventually falls to the feet of Andy Carroll whose low shot is deflected past the keeper on its way into the back of the net.

28 December 2014

Papiss Cisse brings United level with Everton at St James' Park. Trailing to a goal from Toffees striker Arouna Kone, the Magpies make it 1-1 thanks to Mike Williamson's persistence, with the defender somehow salvaging a ball that looked destined to go into touch before finding Cisse who fires the cross home with a precise shot.

35

12 February 1972

Newcastle record a first away win against Manchester United for 22 years with a goal in each half at Old Trafford. The opener comes ten minutes before the break as Stewart Barrowclough gets to the byline on the right before sending a pinpoint cross into the six-yard box where John Tudor arrives to fire past keeper Alex Stepney with a shot into the roof of the net from close range.

28 February 1976

United equalise in the 1976 League Cup Final against Manchester City at Wembley. Having fallen behind on 11 minutes to Peter Barnes's opening goal, the Magpies level when Malcolm Macdonald is played in on the right of the City box – he crosses low into the six-yard box for Alan Gowling to prod a left-foot shot past Joe Corrigan and make the score 1-1. Sadly for United, boyhood Magpies supporter Dennis Tueart spectacularly scores the winner just after the restart with an overhead kick that proves to be the winner for City.

21 October 1995

United go 2-0 up with a second goal in four minutes against Wimbledon. The first goal had been a cross into the box from the right and a header into the left corner – the second goal is a cross from the left and a header into the right of the net. David Ginola whips in a cross and Les Ferdinand powers home to put the Toon in the driving seat against Joe Kinnear's out-of-sorts side.

12 May 2013

More calamitous defending by QPR gifts United the lead at Loftus Road in a vital relegation clash. Jose Bosingwa – guilty of giving a penalty away earlier in the half – receives the ball from keeper Rob Green and his under-hit return pass sees the keeper's attempt to clear charged down by Jonas Gutierrez, and Yoan Gouffran is the beneficiary, stroking the loose ball into the empty net for what will prove the winning goal and ensures United's Premier League survival with one game remaining.

36

22 October 1994

United's superb start to the 1994/95 season continues as Steve Watson fires the Magpies into a 1-0 lead against Sheffield Wednesday. Having won eight and drawn two of the first ten games, Kevin Keegan's side are on the crest of a wave and Watson's 36th-minute strike has all of St James' Park on their feet as he collects a pass on the edge of the box from Lee Clark before stepping inside a challenge and thumping a rising shot past the keeper inside the left-hand post.

26 February 2003

Alan Shearer completes his first Champions League hat-trick and his first Newcastle United treble for four years to put the Magpies 3-0 up in the group stage clash with Bayer Leverkusen at St James' Park. Shearer had already bagged a brace of headers in the first 11 minutes and he is presented with a chance to claim the match ball when Kieron Dyer is blatantly tugged back in the box by Thomas Kleine, resulting in a penalty being awarded. Shearer emphatically blasts the spot kick into the top right-hand corner in a game that United eventually win 3-1.

22 July 2006

United go 2-0 up in the second leg of the Intertoto Cup against Lillestrom in Norway. The goal comes when Stephen Carr sets Scott Parker free down the right flank and his low cross into the six-yard box is met by Shola Ameobi who makes no mistake from close range for his second goal in seven minutes.

37

23 April 1932

Controversy as Newcastle United level the scores in the 1932 FA Cup Final, leading the game to be later dubbed the 'Over the Line Final'. Trailing 1-0 at Wembley to Arsenal, Jimmy Boyd chases a ball to the byline before sliding a low cross into the middle for Jack Allen to prod home the equaliser. Arsenal players protested long and hard that the ball had gone out of play, but TV replays were inconclusive and – thankfully – Allen's goal stood.

11 May 1968

United hit back quickly again against champions-elect Manchester City. Having earlier pegged City back within 90 seconds of falling behind, this time United are behind for just five minutes as a poor clearance is intercepted by the Magpies and a ball is played up to Bryan Robson on the edge of the box – he runs on to the pass before hitting a first-time half-volley into the top-right corner from 20 yards out to make it 2-2 in a roller-coaster match at St James' Park.

22 October 1994

The Magpies make it two goals in the space of a minute against Sheffield Wednesday. Having won possession straight away from the kick-off, United attack down the left and keeper Kevin Pressman comes out of his box to clear – but his weak effort goes to Scott Sellers who skips past him and manages to send a deep cross into the six-yard box where Andy Cole expertly diverts the ball into the unguarded net, despite the presence of two Owls defenders either side of him. The 2-0 lead will be enough to secure victory (2-1 at the final whistle) and means the on-fire Toon have taken 29 out of a possible 33 points at the start of the 1994/95 campaign.

7 April 2005

United get a vital first-leg goal against Sporting Lisbon in the UEFA Cup quarter-final, to take a 1-0 lead back to Portugal. Inevitably, Alan Shearer is the scorer, finding acres of space in the Lisbon box to power a header past Ricardo courtesy of a fine Laurent Robert free kick. Crucially, the Magpies manage to keep a clean sheet as well as Graeme Souness looks to guide United to a first European final since the Inter-Cities Fairs Cup triumph of 1969, some 36 years earlier.

38

9 September 1972

A Stewart Barrowclough corner is scrambled clear by the Arsenal defence, but only to the edge of the box where a low shot is fired in and diverted past the keeper into the net by the predatory Malcolm Macdonald from five yards out to put Newcastle 1-0 up against the Gunners at a sunny and noisy St James' Park.

39

9 January 1988

Paul Gascoigne demonstrates his undoubted genius yet again as he scores what will be the only goal of the game against Crystal Palace. The 20-year-old picks up the ball midway inside the Crystal Palace half before letting fly with a 30-yard shot that curls into the top-left corner of the net to put the Magpies 1-0 up and settle the FA Cup third-round tie at St James' Park.

23 January 1988

For the second home game running, Paul Gascoigne scores the opening goal for Newcastle at St James' Park. Having scored a wonderful long-range effort a fortnight earlier, Gazza's goal against Spurs is less spectacular, but equally as important. Darren Jackson's cross into the box from the left is guided home by Gascoigne from close range for his fourth of the campaign.

26 December 1989

Michael O'Neill scores a somewhat lucky winner for United away to Sheffield Wednesday on Boxing Day 1989 – not that anyone in black and white (or yellow and green on this occasion) was complaining. A Kevin Brock cross from the left is nodded into the path of O'Neill and, as the Northern Ireland striker stumbles, he mishits the ball, which fools the keeper who watches in agony as it rolls into the bottom-right corner to end a run of four successive away defeats.

21 September 2002

Alan Shearer doubles United's lead against Sunderland to send St James' Park into dreamland. After Jason McAteer concedes a free kick 20 yards out, Shearer, heavily bandaged around his head from an earlier injury, steps up to thump a powerful drive past the Black Cats keeper Thomas Sorensen and condemn beleaguered Sunderland boss Peter Reid to a 2-0 defeat.

21 December 2013

Newcastle double their lead at a rainy Selhurst Park thanks to Crystal Palace defender Danny Gabbidon. Mathieu Debuchy fizzes a low cross into the Palace box and Loic Remy pulls back thinking he won't reach it – but Gabbidon is unaware the threat has diminished and his desperate attempt to clear results in putting the ball past his own keeper to make it 2-0 for United.

10 November 2018

A goal that Jackie Milburn, Malcolm Macdonald and Alan Shearer would all have been proud of as Salomon Rondon puts the Magpies 2-0 up against Bournemouth. Play switches from right to left as a cross-field ball finds Kenedy – the Brazilian controls the pass, then whips in a superb cross into the box where Rondon arrives perfectly on cue to thump a header into the top-left corner of the net. It will prove a winning goal, too, despite the Cherries pulling one back, to lift Rafa Benitez's team further away from trouble.

40

9 May 1993

It keeps getting worse for Leicester City who concede a fifth goal before half-time to the rampant Magpies. Andy Cole scores his second of the afternoon as strike partner David Kelly nods down a long ball and Cole sweeps a low shot that takes a slight deflection on its way into the bottom-left corner of the net to make it 5-0.

21 October 1995

Game, set and match for the Magpies who go 3-0 up before the break against Wimbledon. The duo who were responsible for the opening goal combine again to further punish the Wombles as Keith Gillespie skips past the left-back before whipping the ball towards the six-yard box where Les Ferdinand steals in between the keeper and a defender as he stoops to head the ball, which seems to loop up off the back of his head, over the goalie and into the back of the net for his second of the game.

41

10 December 1988

John Hendrie ends United's run of 588 minutes without a goal as he breaks the deadlock against Wimbledon at St James' Park. In manager Jim Smith's first home game, Hendrie plays a neat one-two on the edge of the Dons' box before toe poking the return past the keeper to the great relief of everyone connected with the club.

2 February 2013

United go ahead just before the break against Chelsea. Yohan Cabaye sprays a pass out to the left for Davide Santon who cuts inside his marker before sending a cross towards the penalty spot and Jonas Gutierrez leaps to get the merest glance on the ball but it is enough to direct in low and to the left of Petr Cech to make it 1-0 at St James' Park.

42

23 August 1975

One of the greatest goals St James' Park has ever witnessed, but as no TV cameras were present for the First Division clash with Leicester City, only the 36,084 inside the ground were lucky enough to see it as it happened. Leading 1-0 and with half-time just a few minutes away, United counter-attack at speed. The Foxes have a corner that is cleared by Pat Howard and Irving Nattrass is first to the loose ball and sprints forward. Malcolm Macdonald, having been on the near post to defend the corner, sprints upfield as well and suddenly, with Nattrass on the right and Macdonald running about 12 yards behind, it was now a two versus one situation. The one Leicester player defending on the halfway line decides to half close down Nattrass resulting in a square ball to Macdonald who arrives perfectly on cue to crack a first-time shot from 40 yards out that steadily rises like a missile to a height of five feet and past the keeper to make it 2-0 and secure victory for the hosts. An extraordinary goal from an extraordinary striker.

29 September 1984

Newcastle take the lead against West Ham United in a home First Division clash at St James' Park. Chris

Waddle carries the ball into the Hammers' half before spotting Peter Beardsley out wide on the left flank. Beardsley takes on the right-back, then drops his shoulder, cuts inside and fires a low shot from the edge of the box that takes the merest of deflections on its way to nestling in the bottom-left corner of the net to make it 1-0.

19 September 1999

Alan Shearer completes a 12-minute hat-trick to put United 4-0 up against Sheffield Wednesday. The move starts with a lofted pass from Temuri Ketsbaia to Kieron Dyer on the left – the England international takes the pass into his stride before crossing into the middle where Shearer shows greater desire and hunger to force the ball home from close range, despite the attention of two Wednesday defenders. It all but seals three points in Sir Bobby Robson's first home game in charge with the game not even at half-time.

11 March 2003

Craig Bellamy is the architect as United take the lead in a crucial Champions League group stage clash away to Inter Milan. The Wales international breaks down the right with pace, takes on and skips around an Inter defender before sending a precision low cross into the box for Alan Shearer to convert from close range. The Magpies need victory over Inter to have a chance of moving to the knock-out phase with Barcelona already through.

12 January 2016

Georginio Wijnaldum pulls a goal back for Newcastle three minutes before the break to make it 1-2 in Manchester United's favour. Fabricio Coloccini's dink into the box sees Aleksandar Mitrovic get above two defenders, nod the ball down and Wijnaldum sweeps home a low side-foot volley from ten yards to bring the struggling Magpies back into the game at St James' Park.

43

27 August 1997

Leading Croatia Zagreb 2-1 on aggregate in the Champions League second qualifying round, second leg, United get a vital away goal just before half-time when Jon Dahl Tomasson runs through on goal before being brought down as he tries to go around the goalkeeper. A penalty is awarded and the keeper is shown the red card, allowing Faustino Asprilla – himself fortunate not to have been sent off for blatantly elbowing a Zagreb player earlier in the half – to thump the spot kick high into the top-left corner to make it 1-0. A man advantage and an aggregate lead of 3-1, the Magpies look to have the game sewn up ...

26 August 2001

Craig Bellamy equalises for the Magpies in the 132nd Tyne–Wear derby at St James' Park. With Newcastle trailing 1-0 to Kevin Phillips's 34th-minute opener, Laurent Robert's 40-yard pass sees Bellamy race into the box on an angle with Sunderland's Emerson Thome – the Welsh forward manages to fire a shot that somehow squeezes past Thomas Sorensen to make it 1-1 and earn a draw for Sir Bobby Robson's side.

44

21 August 1971

Having just seen Liverpool miss a penalty at one end, the Magpies go up the other end and take the lead. It is Malcolm Macdonald who does the damage, scoring his second goal of the game on his home debut. The former Fulham and Luton Town striker receives a pass from Terry Hibbitt on the corner of the Liverpool box, where he spins around and nudges the ball past defender Larry Lloyd before firing a thunderous angled shot past Ray Clemence and into the roof of the net from 15 yards out to send St James' Park wild.

14 February 1976

Malcolm Macdonald scores arguably his greatest-ever Newcastle United goal to put the Magpies 2-1 up against Bolton Wanderers in the FA Cup fifth-round tie at Burnden Park. In a previously practised routine, Macdonald would receive the ball from the throw on his right side rather than his favoured left. As the ball comes to him on the left of the Bolton box, Supermac lets it run past him before turning and lashing a ferocious right-foot shot into the top-right corner and gives keeper Barry Siddal no chance. A wonderful strike from one of the Toon's greatest strikers.

24 February 1996

Despite struggling Manchester City's overall dominance, the hosts had failed to add to their 1-0 lead and paid the price on 44 minutes when Belgian centre-half Philippe Albert volleys home a cracking drive from ten yards. Faustino Asprilla is the creator, deftly chipping a pass off Kit Symons's head and into the path of Albert who hits a shot on the up but expertly controls the ball and takes keeper Eike Immel by surprise.

2 October 1999

Another Alan Shearer goal – his tenth in just four games – puts United firmly in control against Middlesbrough at St James' Park. Shearer, who had earlier headed United ahead, doubles the lead as he again powers a headed effort past the Boro keeper to make it 2-0 just on half-time. It will be enough to secure a 2-1 win at St James' Park over the Teessiders.

26 December 2013

Loic Remy makes up for missing a penalty moments earlier by levelling the scores against Stoke City. The visitors had led from the 29th minute but had Glenn Whelan and Marc Wilson sent off within the space of three minutes to swing the advantage firmly Newcastle's way, and Remy's equaliser – a shot high into the middle of the net and assisted by Hatem Ben Arfa – is the start of a long afternoon for the Potters.

45

4 February 1984

Brilliant combination play between Kevin Keegan and Peter Beardsley doubles United's lead away to Portsmouth. Keegan nips in ahead of a challenge on the left before crossing into the box where Beardsley just nicks it past the keeper, sends one defender on to his backside on the line and then dummies a shot past another before calmly slotting into the empty net to double the Magpies' lead at Fratton Park. Beardsley at his brilliant best.

30 January 1988

Another Paul Gascoigne special puts Newcastle firmly in the driving seat against Swindon Town. With almost 30,000 crammed into St James' Park for the FA Cup fourth-round tie, Darren Jackson approaches the Robins' box before cleverly slipping a disguised pass to Gascoigne on the left. Gazza feigns a shot, sending a defender sliding on his backside before curling a measured rising drive into the far corner of the net to add to his collection of memorable strikes.

2 May 1992

Knowing a victory would guarantee Second Division survival, the Magpies travelled to Filbert Street to take on a Leicester City side who could still secure the second automatic promotion slot. It was a tall order for Kevin Keegan's revitalised side, but on the stroke of half-time, an attempted back pass by Steve Johnson is intercepted by Gavin Peacock who bides his time before calmly chipping the ball over the advancing keeper from the edge of the box to give United a 1-0 lead at the break.

9 May 1993

David Kelly completes an incredible first half of football at St James' Park as he makes it 6-0 to the Magpies on the stroke of half-time. In a game that few who witnessed it will forget, United were merciless with Kelly bagging a 17-minute hat-trick for the Republic of Ireland striker, he powers a header home from close range following a neat build-up on the right flank. Incredible stuff.

1 January 1994

Andy Cole doubles Newcastle's advantage at home to Manchester City. With the visitors clinging on and fortunate not to be further behind following a controversially disallowed Peter Beardsley goal, City's high defensive line is again breached as Lee Clark clips a lovely ball into space ahead of Cole who races clear and, as the keeper comes to meet him, the prolific No.9 tucks a low shot into the bottom-right corner of the net to put the hosts in a position they will not surrender.

18 September 1994

Having seen his first 'goal' credited to Martin Keown, Peter Beardsley is given the chance to score a goal nobody can erase. Ruel Fox sends a cross into the six-yard box and Philippe Albert is crudely pushed from behind by Lee Dixon, resulting in a stonewall penalty. Beardsley steps up and sends David Seaman the wrong way to put United 2-1 up on half-time at Highbury.

22 December 1999

In an entertaining FA Cup replay, Warren Barton's crosses from the right cause more problems for Spurs as another in-swinger is fumbled by the Spurs keeper and Duncan Ferguson thunders a powerful shot off the underside of the crossbar to restore the injury-ravaged Magpies' two-goal cushion and ensure Sir Bobby Robson's men go in 3-1 up at the break.

30 March 2007

United equalise at White Hart Lane with a rare goal from Nicky Butt. The former Manchester United midfielder – who will only score five goals in 175 appearances for the Toon – receives the ball from Geremi, who picks up on a poor Jonathan Woodgate clearance, and strokes a low shot past Paul Robinson from 20 yards out with the Spurs keeper presumably unsighted as the gentle shot rolls past him and into the bottom-left corner of the net to make it 1-1.

20 April 2008

The Magpies double their lead on the stroke of half-time against Sunderland. Michael Owen runs towards the box before exchanging passes with Mark Viduka – as Owen lifts the ball over Danny Higginbotham, the Black Cats defender almost catches the ball as he slides in giving the referee an easy decision in pointing to the spot. Owen's penalty is a poor one – he hits it straight down the middle without much power – but keeper Craig Gordon makes a hash of it, diving over the ball and allowing it to squeeze underneath him. With no further scoring in the game, United claim a 2-0 victory and banish all fears of relegation, while Sunderland slip further towards the trapdoor.

24 April 2017

United regain the lead on half-time in the vital Championship clash with Preston North End. A swift counter-attack sees Isaac Hayden find Aleksandar Mitrovic on the right of the box – he immediately plays a low ball into the middle and Christian Atsu arrives to place a shot past the keeper and put United 2-1 up.

45+1

3 March 2020

United go 2-0 up in first-half added time, courtesy of a brilliant piece of skill by Joelinton. As an attack down the right flank looks to have fizzled out, the ball falls to Joelinton who instantly back-heels the ball into the middle of the box where Miguel Almiron slides in a shot that rockets into the top-left corner of the West Brom net to double the lead in the FA Cup fifth-round tie.

45+3

31 October 2010

Ecstasy for the sell-out St James' Park crowd as Shola Ameobi puts United 3-0 up in the Tyne–Wear derby. As Jonas Gutierrez dashes into the box, he is fouled by Nedum Onuoha and the referee points to the spot. Ameobi, with four previous goals against Sunderland, steps up to confidently put the ball into the bottom-left corner, just out of the reach of the keeper who had guessed correctly.

Second half

46

11 June 1969

After winning the first leg of the Inter-Cities Fairs Cup against Ujpest Dozsa at St James' Park by a scoreline of 3-0, the Magpies find themselves 2-0 down in the return leg at the Megyeri úti Stadium, Budapest. The next goal would be crucial in terms of which way the tie would swing and, in the first minute of the second half, it was United who scored it. Jackie Sinclair's corner is cleared back to the him on the left and this time his cross is thumped home by skipper Bobby Moncur. It's Moncur's third goal of the contest, having scored a brace in the first leg – his first goals for the club despite having seven years of service under his belt!

4 May 1993

Needing a victory to secure the second-tier title and a return to the top flight, the Toon Army travels in numbers along the east coast to Blundell Park, Grimsby. The Mariners ended the Magpies' 100 per cent start earlier in the season, so United were keen to leave Humberside with all three points and, just 24 seconds after the restart, Andy Cole breaks the deadlock. Rob Lee's drive forward sees the midfielder play a ball into the path of Andy Cole who controls the pass before tucking home from eight yards to give Kevin Keegan's side a 1-0 lead.

19 September 1999

The rout of Sheffield Wednesday continues a minute after the restart as Kieron Dyer puts the rampant Magpies 5-0 up. Dyer, who had already created two goals, is the beneficiary of a move that starts with Alan Shearer playing a short pass into the box for Gary Speed who stumbles as he is about to shoot – but there is enough power to force the keeper to push the ball up towards Shearer who nods it back across the six-yard box for Dyer to head home from a couple of yards out.

47

4 January 2012

A truly stunning free kick from the gifted Yohan Cabaye puts Newcastle 2-0 up against Manchester United at St James' Park. There seems little threat of a direct shot as Cabaye stands alone over the ball, some 30 yards out. But Cabaye spots an opportunity and, supremely confident in his ability, runs up and curls a powerful shot into the top-left corner, off the underside of the crossbar and just out of David de Gea's reach – perhaps the only place he could have put the ball – and in doing so doubles the lead for Alan Pardew's side. Stunning stuff from the French playmaker.

3 March 2020

Valentino Lazaro scores his first goal in English football to seemingly end the FA Cup fifth-round tie at West Brom. In truth, the Inter Milan loanee won't have many simpler goals as Miguel Almiron spots Allan Saint-Maximin on the left of the West Brom box and in space – he hits a low shot that is parried by the keeper, but only into the body of Lazaro who doesn't have to do anything else to ensure the ball crosses the line to make it 3-0 for the Magpies. It also ensures – despite the hosts pulling two goals back to ensure a nervy last few moments – a quarter-final place against Manchester City – the furthest United have got since 2006.

48

17 September 1997

The roof nearly lifts off St James' Park as United go 3-0 up against Barcelona on an unforgettable Champions League night for the Magpies. And just as it had been for the first goal, it is a combination of Keith Gillespie and Faustino Asprilla that rips the Catalans' defence to shreds. Gillespie receives the ball on the halfway line and speeds past the Barca left-back (again) before sending a cross into the middle where Asprilla again times his leap to perfection to thump home his second header of the game and complete his hat-trick, guaranteeing himself a place in the club's folklore as a result. Though the La Liga side pull two goals back, Asprilla's treble is enough to give Kenny Dalglish's side a famous 3-2 win.

26 December 2013

Yoan Gouffran gives the Magpies the lead against nine-man Stoke City at St James' Park. The Magpies quickly look to press their two-player advantage and it results in a second goal just after the break. Hatem Ben Arfa's cross is headed into the air and keeper Thomas Sorensen sees his weak punch land at the feet of Gouffran who sends a low shot into the back of the net to make the score 2-1.

23 April 2016

Trailing 2-0 at Anfield, where United hadn't won in 20 visits, the Magpies are given a lifeline against Liverpool by Papiss Cisse. After a neat build-up down the right flank, the ball is crossed in by Vurnon Anita and, as keeper Simon Mignolet flaps at and misses at the ball, Cisse rises behind him to nod home at the Kop End and halve the deficit against the Reds.

13 September 2016

United go three goals up with a stunning effort from Jonjo Shelvey. Ayoze Perez holds the ball up on the edge of the QPR box before rolling a short pass to Shelvey who moves the ball slightly to the right before curling a sumptuous shot into the top right-hand corner of the net and already seemingly sealing a fifth successive Championship win for Rafa Benitez's side.

49

4 February 1989

Danish defender Frank Pingel puts Newcastle 2-1 up against Liverpool at a wet and windy St James' Park. Pingel heads a corner towards goal from the corner of the six-yard box and it somehow finds its way past two defenders and Bruce Grobbelaar to give bottom of the table United a shock lead.

23 February 1994

Andy Cole gets the first of three goals to put United 1-0 up against Coventry City at St James' Park. Having missed the previous two games through injury – both of which ended in defeats for the Magpies – the Newcastle top scorer shows his predatory instincts as he chases a long ball, pressures the defender into a weak header back and then gets to the ball before the keeper, knocking it over him before running in to finish the job from a yard out as two Coventry players closed in.

11 March 2003

United respond almost immediately to Inter Milan's equaliser at the San Siro in a must-win game for the Magpies. The goal is a result of some poor goalkeeping, with Francesco Toldo flapping at a deep cross from the left flank by Laurent Robert with the ball falling invitingly at the feet of Alan Shearer who bundles a shot into the unguarded net, sending thousands of travelling fans wild. For Shearer, it makes it five goals in two Champions League games – four from open play which, considering he'd scored none from open play prior to that in the competition, was quite a turnaround.

25 October 2004

Laurent Robert claims his first of the season as he breaks the deadlock against Kevin Keegan's Manchester City at St James' Park with a stunning free kick. Nicky Butt's drive towards the City box is ended by a Paul Bosvelt foul with the referee awarding a free kick for the Magpies. Robert is the man who steps up and, even though he slips as he takes it, the Frenchman curls a free kick into the right of the net from 20 yards out with City keeper David James nowhere near to put United ahead in what will be the start of a manic spell of scoring between the teams.

22 September 2010

Shola Ameobi takes full advantage of a sloppy defensive pass to put United 3-1 up against Chelsea at Stamford Bridge. Paulo Ferreira plays a ball square but straight into the path of Ameobi just past the halfway line, but the Newcastle striker still has plenty to do. As defenders converge as he approaches the Chelsea box, Ameobi takes everyone by surprise by curling a low shot past the keeper from 25 yards out to give the Magpies a two-goal cushion in the League Cup tie in West London.

50

28 April 1951

United's exciting side of the 1950s take on Blackpool and the legendary Stanley Matthews in the 1951 FA Cup Final at Wembley. But if the Seasiders had Matthews, the Magpies had Jackie Milburn and it would be Wor Jackie who made the difference on the day and won the battle of two extraordinary talents of the day. After a goalless first half, United go ahead when a prod forward dissects Blackpool's high defensive line allowing Milburn to sprint clear and calmly drill home past George Farm and make it 1-0.

11 June 1969

Preben Arentoft turns the Inter-Cities Fairs Cup Final on its head as he levels the scores against Ujpest Dozsa in the Megyeri úti Stadium, Budapest. Having gone in 2-0 down at the break and seen the first leg 3-0 lead reduced to 3-2 on aggregate, the Magpies resume control with two goals in the first five minutes of the second period. Bobby Moncur had scored on 46 minutes and Danish forward Arentoft makes it 2-2 on the night and 5-2 overall as Jim Scott's shot takes a deflection that loops up and into the path of Arentoft who hits a left volley into the top right-hand corner from eight yards out.

16 November 1974

Paul Cannell continues his knack of scoring goals when called upon to put United 1-0 up against Chelsea. Stewart Barrowclough wins possession back on the right flank and Alan Kennedy takes over, lofting a fine cross to the far post where Cannell rises to nod home.

12 May 1984

Having marked his farewell appearance with the opening goal against Brighton & Hove Albion, Kevin Keegan provides the assist that sees United go 2-1 up on the final day of the 1983/84 campaign. Already guaranteed promotion, the Magpies go back in front when John Trewick lays the ball to Keegan on the right flank and his dart forward and cross into the box finds the head of Chris Waddle who nods the ball past the keeper and in off the post. It is the winger's 18th of the season, but a rare headed effort.

26 October 1988

A superb free kick puts United 2-0 up against Middlesbrough at St James' Park. Mirandinha, who had been causing Boro problems throughout the game, stands over a free kick on the left of the Teessiders' box. The ball is touched to him and he drills a low shot into the bottom right of the net from 22 yards out to the delight of the Newcastle supporters, desperate to see their struggling side move off the bottom of Division One.

Jackie Milburn in action in the 1952 FA Cup Final v Blackpool – 'Wor Jackie' scored 201 goals for United in 399 matches.

Malcolm Macdonald celebrates his second goal against Liverpool on his home debut in August 1971.

Supermac opens the scoring against Burnley in March 1974 to put the Magpies 1-0 up in the FA Cup semi-final.

Supermac, doing what he did best, with a subtle low drive to put United 2-0 up against Burnley in the March 1974 FA Cup semi-final at Hillsborough – his second of the game.

Kevin Keegan marks his Newcastle debut with the only goal of the game against QPR in August 1982.

Faustino Asprilla scores from the penalty spot during an unforgettable Champions League clash with Barcelona in September 1997.

Faustino Asprilla completes his hat-trick against Barcelona on an electric night at St James' Park in September 1997.

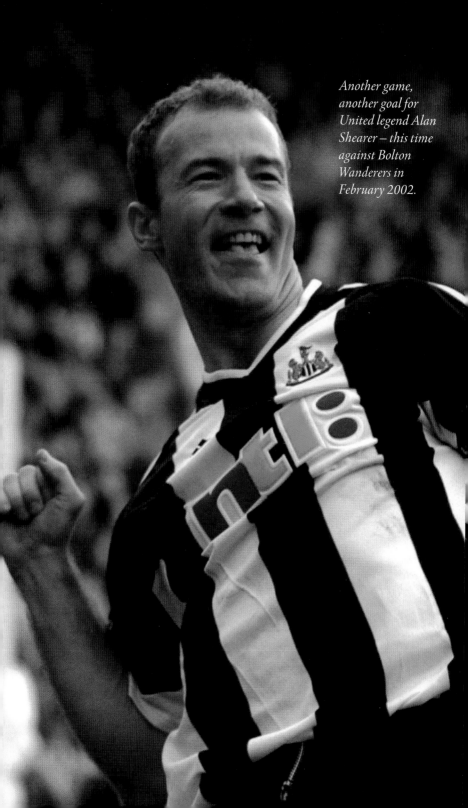

*Another game,
another goal for
United legend Alan
Shearer – this time
against Bolton
Wanderers in
February 2002.*

Alan Shearer's iconic celebration in all its glory as he scores the opener against Manchester United.

Wearing a protective mask, Shola Ameobi shows there's nothing wrong with his eyesight as he bags a goal against Wolves in April 2011.

Yohan Cabaye on target against Manchester United in December 2013.

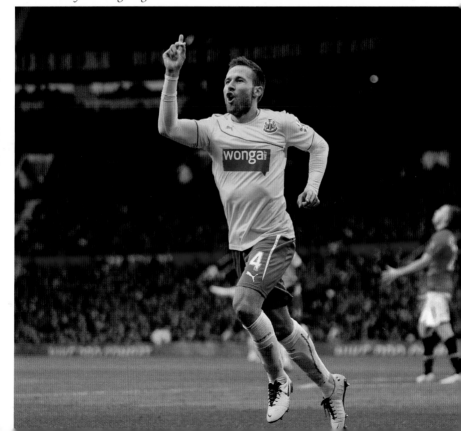

Andy Carroll and Matty Longstaff celebrate the latter's winning goal against Manchester United in October 2019.

15 July 2006

A rare moment of joy for Spanish striker Albert Luque as he brings United level in the Intertoto Cup third-round first leg at St James' Park. With Newcastle trailing 1-0 to Norwegian side Lillestrom, Luque takes the ball to the edge of the box before curling an exquisite left-foot shot around a defender and the goalkeeper to make it 1-1 in front of a sun-drenched crowd of 31,059.

51

21 August 1994

Andy Cole opens his and Newcastle's account for the 1994/95 campaign in the opening fixture away to Leicester City. Peter Beardsley claims an assist as he picks up the ball on the left of the box before drilling a low cross into the six-yard box where the predatory Cole flicks home to make it 1-0 against the Foxes.

28 December 2014

Ayoze Perez – a bargain £1.5m signing from Tenerife – continues to increase his already sizeable fan club as he scores a fine individual goal against Everton. The Toffees had led 1-0 until Papiss Cisse levelled before half-time, and Perez's goal makes it 2-1 as he wriggles past a couple of challenges on the edge of the box before hitting a low drive through the legs of Seamus Coleman and past keeper Joel Robles to edge the Magpies ahead.

52

28 April 1910

Albert Shepherd puts United 1-0 up in the 1910 FA Cup replay against Barnsley. The first game, held at Crystal Palace in London, had ended 1-1 five days earlier, but it is the Magpies who dominate large periods of the replay – this time held at Everton's Goodison Park – and Shepherd delights the north-east contingent of the 60,000 crowd with the opening goal seven minutes after the restart.

7 May 1955

Bobby Mitchell puts United 2-1 up against Manchester City in the FA Cup Final. City, reduced to ten men after an injury to Jimmy Meadows (with no subs back then), had fought back from going behind to Jackie Milburn's first-minute header to go in level at the break. But just seven minutes after the restart, the Magpies are back in front as Len White's deep cross from the right finds Mitchell who controls before hitting a low shot from a tight angle that beats Bert Trautmann on his near post.

28 April 1990

Newcastle are presented with the perfect opportunity to avenge themselves against West Ham United side that had relegated them from the top flight just 12 months earlier. The Magpies, needing a win to guarantee at least a play-off spot in the Second Division, are facing a Hammers side desperate to leave St James' Park with three points to secure their own play-off spot and it is the visitors who took a 1-0 lead into the break, courtesy of a Julian Dicks penalty on 35 minutes. Mark McGhee, in his second spell on Tyneside, is the creator as he dinks a cross to the back post from inside the West Ham box for Bjorn Kristensen to nod home and make it 1-1.

8 November 1993

Andy Cole bags his 17th goal in 16 games as United level the scores against Oldham Athletic at Boundary Park – and it's a stunning effort that gets Kevin Keegan's men back on terms. Cole gets a break when a pass finds its way into his path and, as he bears in on goal, two defenders track back to stop him – he moves to the left of one challenge and then, having spotted the keeper off his line, Cole dinks a shot over the top of the Latics' custodian and into the net from the edge of the box to make it 1-1.

15 September 2001

Sloppy Manchester United defending gives the Magpies a 3-1 lead at St James' Park. A Nolberto Solano corner is half cleared by David Beckham but only to the left of the box where a shot is fired in and is controlled by Nikos Dabizas who spins in between two United defenders and then fires a powerful drive high into the roof of the net from six yards out to put Newcastle 3-1 up.

30 March 2007

If the equalising goal against Spurs had looked soft, keeper Paul Robinson again had questions to answer as United go 2-1 up at White Hart Lane. Awarded a free kick some 20 yards out, Geremi stands alone over the ball before hitting a low shot around the left of the wall and finding the bottom-left corner of the net with Robinson rooted to the spot.

53

16 January 1994

A magical goal from Peter Beardsley restores United's lead at Loftus Road. Lee Clark's attempted pass from the right is cut out by a QPR defender, but Beardsley quickly wins the ball back and passes to Andy Cole on the edge of the box before lashing in a superb volley from Cole's return pass to give keeper Tony Roberts no chance – it will prove to be the winning strike, too, as Kevin Keegan's side head north after a 2-1 victory.

10 September 1994

For the third time of the afternoon, Newcastle take the lead against Chelsea in an entertaining clash at St James' Park. The visitors had twice pegged back Kevin Keegan's side but, each time, United had an answer and this time it is a neat combination in the box between Ruel Fox and Rob Lee that makes it 3-2 to the hosts. Fox receives a ball into the box from the left and plays a simple pass on to Lee who side-foots past Dmitri Kharine from six yards out.

4 September 1997

In the last-ever Tyne–Wear derby at Roker Park, Sunderland lead 1-0. With only home fans allowed for the final campaign at Roker, more than 8,000 Newcastle fans watch the game live from the Newcastle Arena and, seven minutes after the break, they are celebrating as Les Ferdinand gets to the right of the Black Cats' box before lifting a cross into the middle where Peter Beardsley heads the ball just inside the left post and out of the goalkeeper's reach to make it 1-1.

54

3 February 1996

Kevin Keegan's rampant Newcastle take the lead against Sheffield Wednesday at St James' Park. Chasing a 13th successive home win, the opening goal comes via a Keith Gillespie corner which meets the head of Philippe Albert – he nods towards goal and Les Ferdinand powers the ball over the line for his 23rd of the season and to put the Magpies 1-0 up.

24 May 2015

United went into the final day of the 2014/15 campaign knowing a victory would guarantee Premier League survival while relegating Hull City. Bizarrely, the same scenario had occurred six years earlier, with the Magpies going down and Hull staying up – so this was a chance for revenge. The opening goal comes when Jonas Gutierrez sends a deep cross into the West Ham box and Moussa Sissoko leaps higher than those around him to nod down powerfully and beat the keeper, to the delight of the sell-out St James' Park crowd.

20 November 2016

The Magpies double their lead at Elland Road to silence a large portion of the 36,000 sell-out crowd. Vurnon Anita is the creator, playing a one-two on the edge of the box before sending in a perfect low cross for Dwight Gayle to place the ball past Rob Green and claim his second that afternoon. With no further goals, United head home with a 2-0 win and move five points clear at the top of the Championship.

55

28 April 1951

The brilliant Jackie Milburn scores his second goal in five minutes to effectively seal victory for United in the 1951 FA Cup Final. Despite Blackpool having Stanley Matthews and Stan Mortensen in their ranks, it is Wor Jackie who steals the show, firing a bullet of a shot into the top right-hand corner from distance to secure a 2-0 victory at Wembley and a fourth FA Cup success for the Magpies.

3 May 1995

In an astonishing seesaw battle at St James' Park, the Magpies find themselves on the brink of a damaging Premier League loss at home to Tottenham. Having led 2-0 after just ten minutes, Spurs rally to score three in six first-half minutes to edge 3-2 in front. But things look to be very much swinging Spurs' way when Nick Barmby breaks through and, as he goes around keeper Pavel Srnicek, he is brought crashing to the turf and a penalty is awarded. Worse still, Srnicek is then shown the red card and United are reduced to ten men. Ruel Fox makes way for sub keeper Mike Hooper, whose first task is to face Jurgen Klinsmann from the penalty spot. With the Toon fans at fever pitch, Klinsmann's shot down the middle is saved by Hooper's trailing foot and the roof almost comes off the stadium. Incredible stuff and an incredible game that still has a couple more twists to come ...

56

23 January 1988

Paul Gascoigne scores his second of the game against Spurs – and perhaps convinces the North London club that they have to have him in their squad, no matter what the cost. After Newcastle are awarded a free kick on the edge of the Spurs box, the ball is touched to Gazza who manages a sort of golf shot – chipped with power and curl – and into the top-left corner to seal a 2-0 victory and further enhance his rocketing reputation.

28 April 1990

St James' Park erupts as United go 2-1 up against West Ham in a crucial promotion battle. Having only levelled four minutes earlier, the Magpies have the momentum, and goalscorer Bjorn Kristensen carries the ball into the Hammers half before finding Liam O'Brien on the right. O'Brien plays a ball to the feet of Mick Quinn in the box and the Newcastle striker – with his back to goal – controls and spins away from his marker before firing a shot that is blocked, but the ball falls invitingly back to Quinn who sends a thunderous volley into the roof of the net from six yards.

16 April 1994

A superb counter-attack puts United 2-0 up at Anfield. Just seconds before, Liverpool had half-heartedly claimed for a penalty, but Pavel Srnicek immediately releases a throw to Scott Sellars who sends Ruel Fox into acres of space on the right flank. Fox powers forward before playing a precise ball between two Liverpool defenders and into the path of Andy Cole who takes one touch before drilling a low right-foot shot past David James and into the bottom-left corner of the net to send the Toon Army into raptures. With no further scoring, it is the Magpies' second successive league win at Anfield having waited 38 years for a victory in this fixture prior to the first of those back-to-back wins on Merseyside.

26 December 2013

Loic Remy scores his second goal of the game as Newcastle go 3-1 up against nine-man Stoke. The Potters, clearly intent on damage limitation, sink deeper and deeper in their own half as they focus on keeping the score down, but when Davide Santon's cross is flicked on by Moussa Sissoko, Remy heads home to all but seal a Boxing Day victory, despite there being almost 35 minutes to play.

13 September 2016

Matt Ritchie claims his second assist of the game as United go 4-0 up at Loftus Road. The simplest of the goals scored so far, Ritchie swings in a corner from the right and Ciaran Clark rises highest to nod the ball into the bottom-left corner from close range to seal victory with less than an hour played.

57

3 April 1996

Just two minutes after Liverpool had drawn level at 2-2, the Magpies restore the lead in a classic Premier League encounter at Anfield. With the home fans still celebrating Robbie Fowler's goal, Rob Lee threads a pass through to Faustino Asprilla who times his run to perfection – as the keeper races out of his box he strikes a shot with the outside of his right foot that beats the goalie easily to make it 3-2 for Kevin Keegan's side.

58

21 August 1994

United double their lead away to Leicester City on the opening day of the 1994/95 campaign. Having created the first goal, Peter Beardsley scores the second himself, collecting a pass on the edge of the Foxes' box, before shimmying his way past one challenge and drilling a low shot past the keeper to put Kevin Keegan's side 2-0 up at Filbert Street.

29 December 2002

United's sustained pressure finally leads to a deserved second goal in the clash with Spurs at St James' Park. With Newcastle leading from Gary Speed's first-half goal, Craig Bellamy receives the ball and the Tottenham defence give him too much time to send a measured cross to Alan Shearer who buries a header into the net at the far post to make it 2-0 and put the Magpies firmly in control and on the way to a 2-1 win that will move Sir Bobby Robson's men up to fourth spot in the Premiership.

25 October 2004

A swashbuckling run from full-back Stephen Carr ends with a penalty for United against Manchester City. The Irish defender stumbles as he chases a pass and is caught by Steve McManaman and then, as he nicks it past keeper David James, he is felled in the box and the spot kick is awarded. Alan Shearer blasts the ball into the top-right corner to make it 2-0 against Kevin Keegan's men – though the scoring is far from over in what will become a minor classic of an encounter.

59

21 October 1995

Wimbledon are made to pay immediately for having their goalkeeper sent off for a second bookable offence. Paul Heald is way out of his goal on the right flank as he cleans out Les Ferdinand and the referee sends him for an early bath. Down to ten men, Vinnie Jones takes over in net and within a few seconds he is watching Lee Clark's howitzer into the top-left corner from 20 yards out to make it 4-0 and, in fairness, not many real goalkeepers could have stopped Clark's shot.

21 September 1996

Alan Shearer scores what will be the only goal of the game as the Magpies beat Leeds United 1-0 at Elland Road for the second time in 11 games. Having beaten the Lilywhites towards the end of the previous campaign by the same score, Kevin Keegan's side make the 100-mile trip down the A1 again and, with the hosts reduced to ten men after Carlton Palmer's first-half dismissal, Shearer bags the winner just before the hour mark as he races on to Rob Lee's clever pass before firing a low shot past the keeper from 15 yards out for his fourth of the campaign.

28 December 1996

Les Ferdinand grabs his second goal against future employers Spurs to all but wrap up victory with less than an hour played at St James' Park. The Magpies go 3-0 up as Peter Beardsley plays the ball to the overlapping John Beresford and his deep cross to the back post is met on the volley by Ferdinand from close range to give the keeper no chance and condemn the North London side to defeat.

14 May 2000

Wales international Gary Speed grabs his second goal of the game and his 13th of the season to once again restore the Magpies' lead in a seesaw battle at St James' Park. There are no airs or graces about the goal – Nolberto Solano sends in a corner and Speed thumps a header downwards and then sees the ball bounce up into the roof of the net to give keeper Alex Manninger no chance and makes it 3-2 for United.

7 May 2017

United double their lead against Barnsley at St James' Park. With Newcastle needing a win to have any chance of being crowned champions of the Championship, the ball finds its way to Ayoze Perez who sees a fierce shot saved by the keeper – but the ball only comes out to Chancel Mbemba who thumps the loose ball home to make it 2-0.

13 May 2018

United double their lead against Chelsea with the deftest of flicks from Ayoze Perez. When the ball comes out to Jonjo Shelvey 25 yards out, he hits a stinging low drive that arrows towards goal – and the feet of Perez – who gets the merest of touches to help the ball into the bottom-left corner of the net with Chelsea keeper Thibaut Courtois nowhere near to keeping it out.

60

7 May 1955

Brilliant wing play by Bobby Mitchell allows United to take a two-goal advantage of ten-man Manchester City in the 1955 FA Cup Final. With Newcastle leading 2-1, Mitchell receives the ball on the right of the City box before bamboozling the right-back and dribbling into the box where his low cross is touched away by Bert Trautmann but only into the path of George Hannah who drills home from eight yards to make it 3-1 and ultimately seal victory for Doug Livingstone's team.

26 August 1982

St James' Park is fit to burst as United fans cram in to watch the debut of football superstar Kevin Keegan. Signed for just £100,000 from Southampton, it will prove to be an inspirational move by Newcastle with near-hysteria greeting Keegan's arrival on Tyneside. And, of course, he marks his first game in black and white by scoring the only goal of the game against Queens Park Rangers, collecting Imre Varadi's knockdown before driving towards the box and slipping the ball to the right of the keeper, then diving into the Gallowgate End to celebrate with the supporters. It will be enough to secure a 1-0 win for Newcastle.

20 March 1993

Trailing 2-0 to Birmingham City at St James' Park, the Magpies revival begins with a huge kick upfield by Pavel Srnicek. David Kelly does well to bring the ball under control and turn it inside where Scott Sellars takes over and passes to his right where Andy Cole arrives to prod the ball home from six yards and halve the deficit.

7 April 1998

Alan Shearer books United a place in the FA Cup Final for the first time in 24 years as he bags his fifth goal of the competition to settle the semi-final clash with Sheffield United at Old Trafford. The goal comes as Shearer thumps John Barnes's cross towards goal and though Blades' keeper Alan Kelly keeps the effort out, Shearer is first to the loose ball to force home the winner.

17 April 2006

Michael Chopra scores after coming on just 15 seconds earlier to bring United level in the Tyne–Wear derby. Chopra chases a long punt into the Sunderland box with defender Steven Caldwell allowing him to run clear, perhaps expecting keeper Kelvin Davis to collect the ball or clear it. Chopra then collides with Davis – fairly in the referee's eyes – and the ball falls to him almost on the goal line and he prods home after checking the officials had given it and makes it 1-1.

12 May 2019

A Matt Ritchie corner again results in a goal as the former Bournemouth man floats a cross into the middle of the Fulham box and Fabian Schar rises higher than anyone else to nod the ball down into the bottom-right corner and give United a 3-0 lead at Craven Cottage on the last day of the 2018/19 season.

61

28 December 1996

For the second time in the game, United grab two goals in quick succession to further rub salt in Tottenham's wounds at St James' Park. Lee Clark plays a short ball to Alan Shearer on the left and he, in turn, plays in field to Rob Lee. As space opens up ahead of him, Lee bursts towards the box, dances inside a couple of challenges before planting a right-foot shot into the bottom-left of the net from 18 yards out to make it 4-0.

7 December 2013

Newcastle leave Old Trafford with a famous and long-awaited victory. The Magpies hadn't won away to Manchester United since 1972, but against an out-of-sorts Reds, what will prove to be the only goal of the game arrives just past the hour mark. Moussa Sissoko breaks down the right flank and his pulled-back cross finds Yohan Cabaye who fires the ball past David de Gea for the winning strike.

62

28 April 1910

Albert Shepherd grabs his second goal of the game as United take a firm grip on the 1910 FA Cup Final replay against Barnsley at Everton's Goodison Park. Shepherd, who had put the Magpies ahead just ten minutes earlier, converts from the penalty spot to give Frank Watt's side breathing space in a game where Barnsley's overly physical approach is punished in the best possible manner. There will be no further scoring as the name of Newcastle United is etched on the FA Cup winner's plinth for the very first time.

29 May 1969

Newcastle take the lead against Ujpest Dozsa in the first leg of the Inter-Cities Fairs Cup Final at St James' Park. In front of a packed house of more than 60,000, a free kick is awarded 30 yards from goal. The ball is chipped towards Wyn Davies who connects from close range only for the keeper to push the shot out – but only as far as Bobby Moncur, who drills a low drive into the back of the net to make it 1-0.

20 March 1993

Two goals in two minutes sees St James' Park erupt in a Second Division clash with Birmingham City. Just before the hour mark, Blues had led 2-0, but Andy Cole's goal sparked the Magpies into life and within two minutes, the score is 2-2. Scott Sellars, buoyed up by the home fans, races down the left before sending in a cross into the box for Rob Lee who expertly guides a low shot into the bottom-right corner to send the Gallowgate End wild. It will be enough to earn a crucial point for the promotion-chasing Magpies.

20 October 1996

The Magpies go 3-0 up against Manchester United with another stunning goal. David Ginola's first-half howitzer had doubled Newcastle's lead but, with Manchester United piling the pressure on, Les Ferdinand puts the game almost out of the visitors' reach as Alan Shearer turns provider, beating the left-back on the flank before whipping in the perfect cross into the six-yard box for Ferdinand to power a header in off the underside of the bar before the ball bounces high up and hits the woodwork again before fans realise it has crossed the line.

4 September 1997

Les Ferdinand rises to head home a corner and literally silence Roker Park as United go 2-1 up in the Tyne–Wear derby. With no Newcastle fans present owing to Sunderland restricting access to home fans only for the final season at the stadium, Ferdinand heads a Peter Beardsley cross down and past Tony Coton to ensure it is the Magpies who have the last say in this fixture at Roker Park.

17 April 2006

The travelling Newcastle fans see their side go from 1-0 down to 2-1 up within 65 seconds at the Stadium of Light. United having just levelled through Michael Chopra, Charles N'Zogbia is tugged back in the box by Sunderland's Justin Hoyte and the referee awards a penalty. Playing in his last Tyne–Wear derby, Alan Shearer steps up to blast the spot kick past Kelvin Davis to send the travelling supporters wild.

20 August 2011

In only the second game of the season, Newcastle and Sunderland clash at the Stadium of Light. Having started with a 0-0 draw at home to Arsenal, Alan Pardew's side travel 12 miles down the A1 to take on their greatest rivals on sun-drenched Wearside. What will prove to be the only goal of the game comes when a free kick is awarded on the left of the Sunderland penalty area. Ryan Taylor stands over the ball as players from both sides jostle for position inside the box. Taylor then steps up and fires the free kick over all the heads of his team-mates and into the top-left corner of the net to secure a precious 1-0 victory.

63

21 October 1995

Les Ferdinand completes a hat-trick and sends a message to the England selectors who had left the in-form Toon striker out of the latest squad. Keith Gillespie's cross from the right is nodded down by Lee Clark and Ferdinand sweeps home a low drive that emergency keeper Vinnie Jones does well to get a hand on but the ball still trickles over the line to make it 5-1 against ten-man Wimbledon.

14 May 2000

A special moment for Andy Griffin as he scores his first Newcastle United goal. Rob Lee and Nolberto Solano combine well to give Griffin the opportunity and, faced with Arsenal keeper Alex Manninger, the right-back coolly lifts the ball over and into the back of the net to complete a 4-2 victory on the final day of the season and end Sir Bobby Robson's first season as Magpies boss on a high. The win also lifts United into 13th spot – a remarkable turnaround having taken just one point from a possible 21 at the start of the season.

13 September 2016

Christian Atsu provides the assist as United go 5-0 up away to Queens Park Rangers. The home defence are all at sea when Christian Atsu sends in a low ball from the right to find a totally unmarked Aleksandar Mitrovic in acres of space and the Serbian striker simply side-foots the ball past the keeper from close range.

13 May 2018

A set-piece routine gives the Magpies their third of the afternoon against a poor Chelsea side. Already 2-0 up and cruising, Jonjo Shelvey floats a deep free kick into the box and Florian Lejeune volleys it across the six-yard box for Ayoze Perez to score his second of the game and complete a 3-0 victory. The three points ensure United finish tenth in the table and deny Chelsea a Champions League spot.

64

24 February 2002

In a tense Tyne–Wear derby at the Stadium of Light, the Magpies score what will prove to be the only goal of the game via a set piece. Laurent Robert delivers a cross from the left flank into the box and Alan Shearer gets the merest of touches to help the ball on its way and, as it bounces up, Nikos Dabizas nods home from close range to make it 1-0 and send United back to second in the Premiership.

65

30 March 1974

Malcolm Macdonald shows why there are few better strikers in English football as he puts Newcastle 1-0 up in the FA Cup semi-final against Burnley at Hillsborough. It is a goal borne out of brute strength and determination as Supermac chases a long ball with a Burnley defender attempting to wrestle him to the floor – after shrugging the challenge off, Macdonald fires a shot straight at the keeper which is saved, but as the ball comes back to him, the Magpies' No.9 has the presence of mind to take it between the keeper and a defender before gently rolling a shot past another defender on the line and into the bottom-left corner of the net for his 22nd of the season.

17 December 1989

Manager Jim Smith's decision to take off Mirandinha and replace him with Michael O'Neill proves inspired for a United side trailing 3-1 to Southampton at St James' Park. Brian Tinnion's deep cross from the left falls kindly for O'Neill who lashes a shot into the roof of the net from seven yards to put the Magpies right back in the game.

1 October 1991

A driving run from the halfway line by Liam O'Brien sees the midfielder then split the Tranmere Rovers defence open with a slide rule pass that Gavin Peacock runs on to and strikes past the keeper to put the Magpies 3-2 up at Prenton Park in the Zenith Data Systems Cup.

4 February 1998

Alan Shearer doubles United's lead against non-League Stevenage Borough. The Magpies striker – who scored in the FA Cup fourth-round tie that ended 1-1 and again on 16 minutes in this game – times a diving header perfectly from Rob Lee's cross to make it 2-0 and give the score a more realistic look. Though the Vauxhall Conference minnows will pull one back, Newcastle win 2-1 and move into the last 16 of the competition.

30 March 2007

The Magpies go 3-1 up against Spurs at White Hart Lane with an excellent goal. The hardworking Obafemi Martins is the creator in chief as he battles for possession on the right before playing a low ball in towards Mark Viduka – the Australian steps over the ball which runs on to Michael Owen who curls a shot past Paul Robinson and into the bottom-right corner of the net.

24 April 2017

Paul Gallagher palms away a shot from close range on the goal line for Preston North End – the only issue was he wasn't the keeper! The referee sends Gallagher for an early bath and Matt Ritchie tucks a penalty to the right of the keeper to make it 3-1 and edge United ever closer to promotion from the Championship.

11 February 2018

Matt Ritchie scores the only goal of the game as Newcastle record a first home win for four months against second-placed Manchester United. The Magpies climb several places up the Premier League table, which comes as a result of a free kick for a Chris Smalling dive outside his own box. Jonjo Shelvey's free kick finds Florian Lejeune who nods the ball down; Dwight Gayle flicks it on for Ritchie who has time and space to bury a low shot past David de Gea to secure a precious 1-0 win for Rafa Benitez's men.

3 November 2018

Ayoze Perez scores the goal that gives United a first win of the season. After ten winless games to start the season, the Magpies go into the game against Watford second from bottom in the Premier League, but the relief is palpable as Perez rises to head Ki Sung-yueng's in-swinging free kick to finally beat Hornets keeper Ben Foster and give Rafa Benitez's side a 1-0 win to lift them out of the relegation zone.

9 March 2019

A goal of great invention and execution gets United back into the game against Everton in the Premier League clash at St James' Park. Trailing 2-0 to first-half goals from Dominic Calvert-Lewin and Richarlison, the Magpies – who had earlier seen Matt Ritchie miss a penalty – finally score as Salomon Rondon plays a short pass to Ayoze Perez on the edge of the Toffees' box. Perez then lobs the ball back to Rondon who duly thumps the ball past Jordan Pickford to make it 1-2 – a superb assist from Perez whose influence will become even greater in the time that remains.

66

9 May 1993

Andy Cole becomes the second United player to complete a hat-trick as the Magpies go 7-0 up against beleaguered Leicester City. The Foxes had regrouped somewhat after conceding six first-half goals, but Lee Clark's clever through ball sets Cole clear and the club's record signing drills home a low shot to make it 12 goals in 12 games since arriving from Bristol City. With David Kelly also grabbing a treble, who took the match ball home remains a mystery ...

10 September 1994

Andy Cole's second goal of the game ensures Newcastle's 100 per cent start to the 1994/95 campaign continues. With United leading 3-2 against Chelsea at St James' Park, Rob Lee's burst into the box is thwarted, but he has the presence of mind to play the loose ball to his right inviting Cole to just nip in ahead of a defender and the keeper and slot into the bottom-right corner of the net to make it 4-2 and effectively seal three points for Kevin Keegan's side. It is Cole's sixth goal in five matches.

14 April 2004

Gary Speed sends United into the semi-final of the

UEFA Cup with what proves to be the winning goal against PSV Eindhoven. The Dutch side had equalised to make it 1-1 on the day and 2-2 on aggregate, but Speed powers a Laurent Robert corner home to give United an advantage they won't relinquish. Robert's corners had consistently caused problems for PSV and the French winger claims his second assist of the game.

17 April 2006

The Magpies score their third goal in six minutes with a superb individual goal by the 19-year-old Charles N'Zogbia. Having trailed 1-0 to Sunderland just six minutes before, N'Zogbia further rubs salt into the Black Cats' wounds as he drives at the home defence, evading several challenges before driving a low shot home from 12 yards out.

26 December 2013

United go 4-1 up against nine-man Stoke with a Yohan Cabaye special. With the Potters clinging on and defending deep, clear-cut chances are at a premium, but when Mathieu Debuchy finds Cabaye on the edge of the box, the Magpies' playmaker strikes a low shot into the bottom-right corner from the edge of the box that gives Thomas Sorensen no chance.

23 April 2016

Jack Colback makes it 2-2 away to Liverpool as Rafa Benitez displays the fighting spirit needed to battle relegation. Andros Townsend progresses towards the Reds' box before whipping in a cross from the right that is only half cleared by the home defence and Colback, arriving at the optimum moment, slams home the loose ball from 15 yards to earn a 2-2 draw at Anfield.

29 January 2019

Despite going 1-0 down at home to Manchester City with just 24 seconds played, the Magpies ride their luck and dig in their heels as City continue to create numerous chances. But finally, United fans are on their feet after a poor clearance is nodded back towards the City goal by Isaac Hayden, and Salomon Rondon manages to connect with the ball as it loops back in giving Ederson no chance and making it 1-1.

67

21 August 1971

Malcolm Macdonald caps an incredible home debut by completing his hat-trick against Liverpool. United are good value for a 2-1 lead against a dangerous Liverpool side but Supermac gives the Magpies breathing space when John Tudor cleverly flicks the ball to his right where Macdonald collects, nudges forward and then hits a low left-foot drive into the bottom-right corner of the net to cap an unforgettable first game at St James' Park. It is the start of a prolific spell in black and white for the London-born striker who quickly makes the No.9 shirt his own, though his home bow ends painfully after he is concussed in a clash with Liverpool keeper Ray Clemence.

4 February 1984

Another Kevin Keegan and Peter Beardsley-inspired move ends with a third goal for Newcastle away to Portsmouth. Beardsley sends Keegan clear with a smart through pass but Keegan has to fight off the challenge of Mick Tait as the pair wrestle for possession – Keegan wins and then plays the ball to his left where Beardsley controls before dinking the ball past Alan Knight to make it 3-1 at Fratton Park.

12 March 1994

Having raced into an early 2-0 lead against Swindon Town, the Magpies have to wait almost 50 minutes to add to the scoreline and – in turn – open the floodgates at St James' Park. Andy Cole is played into the right channel of the Swindon box and his low angled shot is pushed out into the path of Rob Lee who bundles the ball home for his second of the afternoon.

4 January 1998

Liverpool legend Ian Rush returns to Merseyside to score yet another goal against Everton as the Magpies look for victory in the FA Cup third-round tie at Goodison Park. The Welsh striker had scored an incredible 25 goals in 36 games for the Reds against the Toffees and it was Rush who was the difference in this tie. Keith Gillespie's cross finds its way to the far post where John Barnes loops the ball back into the six-yard box and master poacher Rush bundles the ball home from close range. An untidy goal, but enough to give Kenny Dalglish's side a 1-0 victory.

22 August 2011

Mike Williamson claims his second assist of the game as United go 4-0 up against Aston Villa. The Magpies defender dinks a hopeful ball into the box from the edge of the penalty area and Andy Carroll reacts quickly to volley home from six yards to seal the points against a woeful Villa side.

12 January 2016

Aleksandar Mitrovic is fouled by Chris Smalling in the box and referee Mike Dean points to the penalty spot. Manchester United had led 2-0 at one stage, but Steve McLaren's side rally and it is Mitrovic – who assisted Wijnaldum's goal – who steps up to calmly stroke home the spot kick and bring the struggling Magpies level.

14 April 2017

United finally break through a stubborn Leeds United defence with a scrappy but vital goal. A deep cross from the right finds Aleksandar Mitrovic who heads across the box from the left and Jamaal Lascelles nods in from close range with his effort just going over the line before being hacked clear. Though Leeds will level deep into stoppage time, it is another point closer to promotion back to the Premier League for the second-placed Magpies.

24 April 2017

United all but seal promotion with a fourth goal of the afternoon against Preston North End. Jonjo Shelvey whips in a curling corner that is missed by everyone and strikes the foot of the far post – the ball bounces back into the middle and Ayoze Perez has the simplest of tasks to put the ball into the empty net to make it 4-1 and confirm a return to the Premier League for the Magpies with two games to spare.

68

2 February 2013

Moussa Sissoko marks his home debut with a goal that makes it 2-2 against Chelsea. A swift counter-attack sees the ball go to Papiss Cisse, just inside his own half. He turns out of trouble and sends Yoan Gouffran clear with two Chelsea defenders desperately trying to catch him. His low shot is saved by Petr Cech but Sissoko is first to the loose ball, turning into the empty net from close range.

2 November 2013

United get the goal they deserve against an in-form Chelsea side to go 1-0 up at St James' Park. The visitors – arriving on the back of six straight Premier League wins – had struck the woodwork twice in the space of a few seconds in the first half but, gradually, the Magpies begin to dominate and are finally rewarded when Yohan Cabaye's excellent free kick from midway inside the Chelsea half finds the head of Yoan Gouffran who powers the ball past Petr Cech for the opening goal of an entertaining game.

28 December 2014

A boyhood dream is realised as Jack Colback bags his first goal for the club he had supported all his life. With

United 2-1 up against Everton, Daryl Janmaat sends a ball into the box and Ross Barkley's poor clearance falls kindly for Colback who makes no mistake from close range to give Alan Pardew's side much-needed breathing space and, despite the Toffees pulling another back six minutes from time, United hold on to win 3-2.

69

19 March 1994

Andy Cole again demonstrates his ability to improvise and score goals from almost anywhere inside the box. Ruel Fox whips a ball in towards the six-yard box and both the West Ham United keeper and defender look odds-on to clear the danger – until Cole wafts a leg out and connects with his studs to divert the ball into the net, put the Magpies 2-1 up at Upton Park and take his season tally up to 36.

25 October 2004

Having seen Manchester City score twice in three minutes to make it 2-2 at St James' Park, United quickly regain the lead in a thrilling encounter. Laurent Robert floats in a free kick from the right and Robbie Elliott's attempt at a back-flick header evades two City defenders, the goalkeeper and Craig Bellamy's attempt to poke home as it hits the post and eventually crosses the line – sadly resulting in a terrible chicken dance celebration from Elliott!

70

12 February 1972

Having made the first goal, Stewart Barrowclough scores the second to give Newcastle a 2-0 lead away to Manchester United. The move starts when George Best appeals for a foul on the right flank, just outside the box – but the referee waves play on and the Magpies break down the left wing. Eventually a cross comes into the six-yard box and Barrowclough drills the ball past Alex Stepney to silence the Stretford End and seal what will be the first win at Old Trafford since 1950.

16 November 1974

A brilliant individual goal doubles Newcastle's lead against Chelsea at St James' Park. Alan Kennedy receives the ball ten yards inside his own half and moves forward with purpose. As he gathers momentum, he runs between two Chelsea defenders before striking a low left-foot shot inside the right post to make it 2-0. A wonderful goal from Kennedy who had run fully 40 yards without being challenged.

20 March 1993

Andy Cole marks his home debut against Notts County with a goal. The Magpies' record signing from Bristol City at £1.75m shows his class, as strike partner David

Kelly chips a ball into his feet and Cole spins and fires a powerful shot past the keeper to put United 4-0 against the other Magpies(!) and ensure the Kevin Keegan steam train continues to power back towards the top flight. It is the first of 68 goals Cole would score for the club in just 84 appearances, paying his transfer fee back many times over.

21 August 1993

Andy Cole becomes the first Newcastle player to score a Premiership goal – and what a stage to do it on. Though the Magpies had scored a goal in the 2-1 midweek loss to Coventry City, it had been an own goal so Cole writes his name into the club's record books as he levels against Manchester United at Old Trafford following a clever lay-off that gave him half a chance in the box – all that he needed – and Cole tucks a low drive inside the right post to earn Kevin Keegan's men a 1-1 draw at defending champions Manchester United. The instinctive striker's name was immediately noted by Reds boss Alex Ferguson ...

23 February 1994

Ruel Fox marks his home debut by being heavily involved in the second goal of the evening against Coventry City. Signed for £2.25m from Norwich City, Fox drives forward down the middle before firing a slightly deflected shot from distance – keeper Steve Ogrizovic pushes the effort out but, inevitably, Andy

Cole is first to the rebound to knock home his second of the night and put the Magpies 2-0 up.

12 March 1994

A dreadful piece of defending from Swindon Town allows Peter Beardsley to seal three points at St James' Park. A Robins defender dithers on the ball as Beardsley presses and then plays an under-hit back pass that allows the United forward to nip in, take it around the keeper and slot home his second of the afternoon and Newcastle's fourth without reply.

3 May 1995

In a thrilling encounter, Newcastle finally level against Spurs. With both teams reduced to ten men and the North London side leading 3-2, a long clearance from just inside the Magpies' half is watched and tracked by Peter Beardsley, who steals in behind Sol Campbell, who misjudges the flight, and controls the ball before firing a right-foot shot powerfully past Ian Walker to make it 3-3 and rescue a point for Kevin Keegan's side.

31 October 2010

Unbridled scenes of joy as United go 4-0 up against Sunderland. Danny Simpson's run down the right and cross finds the head of Andy Carroll who thumps a header against the bar – but with the woodwork still shaking, the ball bounces out to Shola Ameobi on the edge of the box who hits a thunderous rising shot into the roof of the net to guarantee victory in the Tyne–Wear derby at St James' Park as well as claiming his sixth goal against the Black Cats.

5 December 2019

A bizarre but intelligent goal puts Newcastle 2-0 up away to Sheffield United. If ever there was a case for playing to the whistle, this was surely it. As a long ball out of defence finds the head of Andy Carroll, Jonjo Shelvey races on to his flick and is clear on goal – only for the assistant referee to raise his flag for offside. Shelvey decides to see the passage of play through and continues into the penalty area before slotting a low shot past Dean Henderson, who makes a token effort to save the ball. With everyone expecting Shelvey to be booked, the big screens display that a VAR check is in progress. TV replays confirm there was no offside and the VAR awards the goal. It is an extraordinary milestone in the relatively new history of VAR and justifies Shelvey's decision to continue playing. The furious Blades claim to have stopped playing because of the flag, but the referee had clearly waved play on. The goal knocks the stuffing out of the home side and Steve Bruce's men claim three more points as a result.

71

25 November 1995

Trailing 1-0 at St James' Park to Leeds United, the Magpies finally draw level with a superb individual goal from Rob Lee. The England midfielder collects the ball midway inside the Leeds half, but he has a wall of defenders and little support as he heads towards the box. As he jinks one way and then back inside – putting at least one defender on his backside – Lee arrows a low shot from the edge of the box to send Newcastle fans wild.

24 February 1996

Albert, giving a masterful exhibition of attacking defence, pinged in a low cross-shot that Eike Immel could only parry allowing Asprilla – who should have been enjoying an early bath – to screw the ball home from a tight angle for 2-2. It was a bitter pill for the players and the home fans to swallow.

17 April 2006

Alan Shearer leaves the pitch with a medial knee ligament injury and brings to an end his Newcastle United career three games earlier than planned. The Magpies' greatest striker had typically marked his final appearance by scoring what would effectively be the winning goal against Sunderland – fairy-tale stuff – and finishes his career with the Toon. He had made 405 appearances and scores 206 goals in a decade at St James' Park during which time he became a Newcastle United legend.

11 May 2009

Obafemi Martins puts United ahead within seconds of coming off the bench in an inspired Alan Shearer-substitution. Shearer took off Owen with the score at 1-1 against Middlesbrough in a game the Magpies could not afford to lose, and as a loose ball falls his way in the Boro box, Martins spins and fires a low drive past Brad Jones to make it 2-1 in United's favour.

2 May 2010

Peter Lovenkrands scores the goal that gives United victory at Loftus Road and takes Chris Hughton's side to 102 Championship points. On the final day of the campaign and with the title already in the bag, the Magpies are handed a man advantage when Peter Ramage is sent off just 15 seconds after the restart but Neil Warnock's Queens Park Rangers dig in and hold out until 19 minutes from time. Joey Barton's pass sends Lovenkrands clear on goal and, as keeper Radek Cerny races out, the Newcastle striker calmly lofts the ball over his head and into the net for his 16th goal of the season and to seal a 1-0 victory.

28 September 2016

A remarkable comeback begins with Dwight Gayle's second goal of the night against Norwich City at St James' Park. The visitors had recovered from 1-0 down to lead 3-1, but Gayle's goal sparks a breathless fightback. Jonjo Shelvey plays a superb 60-yard pass from his own half into Gayle's path and the former West Brom man controls and volleys home almost in the same movement to make the score 2-3 – it was a wonderful finish but it was a stunning assist from Shelvey.

72

23 April 1932

If United's equaliser against Arsenal in the 1932 FA Cup Final at Wembley had been controversial there were no complaints about the goal that proved to be the winner. Jack Allen's drive towards the Gunners' penalty area sees him draw three defenders before shifting slightly to his left and then firing a low shot into the bottom right-hand corner of the net from the edge of the box. Arsenal, still seething from the Magpies' first-half equaliser that they felt had gone out of play in the build-up, cannot find a response, meaning the FA Cup was heading back to St James' Park for the third time in 22 years.

29 May 1969

Bobby Moncur scores his second goal in ten minutes to send St James' Park wild. Leading 1-0 against Ujpest Dozsa in the first leg of the Inter-Cities Fairs Cup Final, the United skipper picks the ball up on the halfway line before driving forward through the middle. The cultured Scotland international plays a short one-two before continuing his surge and then tries another – but the ball is half-intercepted by a defender who only returns the ball to Moncur who then hits a low left-foot shot into the bottom right-hand corner. A true captain's goal.

25 November 1995

St James' Park goes crazy as Kevin Keegan's United score a second goal in a minute against Leeds United. Having trailed 1-0 up to 70 minutes, the Magpies draw level through Rob Lee and within a minute they take the lead. David Ginola sends in a deep cross from the left flank and Les Ferdinand rises to head the ball towards goal – it's a weak effort, but Leeds keeper John Lukic makes a terrible misjudgement, paws the ball out a couple of yards and Peter Beardsley reacts first to poke the ball into the right corner and score what will be the winning goal in a dramatic 2-1 victory.

6 October 2019

A proud day for Matty Longstaff and Newcastle United manager Steve Bruce as the youngster marks his debut with what will prove to be the only goal of the game against Bruce's former club Manchester United. The 19-year-old keeps his cool as the ball falls to him just outside the Reds' box and drills a low shot past David de Gea to secure a 1-0 victory – the Magpies' first home win of the season – and cap a memorable first game for Longstaff.

73

4 February 1984

Chris Waddle bursts down the left flank and into the Portsmouth box before seeing his low shot beaten out by keeper Alan Knight. Pompey miserably fail to clear the danger and the ball finds its way back to Waddle who then sends a lofted cross towards the back post where Kevin Keegan slides in to volley home his second of the game and complete a 4-1 win at Fratton Park. It is Keegan's 17th of the campaign.

8 November 1993

A Peter Beardsley special puts the Magpies 2-1 up away to Oldham Athletic. The England forward bears towards the Oldham box from the right flank and as the defender commits himself, Beardsley cuts inside and hits a powerful left-foot shot into the top-left corner of the net to give Kevin Keegan's side the lead.

19 March 1994

A superb passing move puts United 3-1 up and in control away to West Ham. Peter Beardsley wins the ball back on the halfway line before zipping a pass to Andy Cole who takes a touch before feeding the overlapping Rob Lee who tucks a low left-foot shot across the keeper and into the bottom-right corner and claims his second of the game. It is also the prolific Cole's second assist of the match.

22 December 1999

Second-half sub Kieron Dyer puts United 4-1 up in an FA Cup third-round replay at St James' Park. Following Alan Shearer's lay-off, Dyer carries the ball into the Spurs box before cleverly passing the ball past the keeper and into the bottom-right corner to all but seal victory for United.

74

11 June 1969

Nineteen-year-old sub Alan Foggon puts the icing on the cake as United seal victory in Hungary against Ujpest Dozsa. The teenager had just come off the bench when he races on to a flick of Willie McFaul's long kick down field and fires a powerful shot that Antal Szentmihályi pushes up and onto the crossbar – but Foggon is first to the rebound, slamming the ball into the back of the net from a yard out to secure a 3-2 win, 6-2 aggregate win and the Inter-Cities Fairs Cup for the jubilant Magpies.

18 September 1994

Peter Beardsley's brilliance results in the Magpies going 3-1 up away to Arsenal. Beardsley – at his tormenting best – picks up a pass just inside the Arsenal half before delightfully jinking around one challenge, then another before firing a shot that strikes a defender and rolls into the path of Ruel Fox who manages to fire a shot from the corner of the six-yard box into the roof of the net from a narrow angle. The Gunners pull one back but United hold on to claim a first win at Highbury since 1987. It also means Kevin Keegan's side have won their first six matches of the season and have a 100 per cent record in the Premier League.

23 December 1995

Rob Lee starts and finishes the move that results in United going 3-1 up against Nottingham Forest. Lee, who scored the opening goal of the game, plays a short pass to the feet of Les Ferdinand on the edge of the Forest box and then gets the ball back as he runs into the box. The pass is slightly behind him but Lee cleverly hooks it into his stride before chipping over Mark Crossley to end the scoring for the afternoon at St James' Park.

20 October 1996

A great day gets even better as Newcastle go 4-0 up against Manchester United. The move starts with Alan Shearer playing a cross-field pass to Peter Beardsley. Beardsley controls the pass, moves towards the edge of the box and fires a powerful shot goalwards. Peter Schmeichel makes a good save, but Les Ferdinand is first to the loose ball, forcing another fine save from the United keeper – but Shearer forces the ball into the bottom-left corner from close range to send St James' Park crazy.

30 September 2000

In a game where both teams squander chances, it is Alan Shearer who finally scores what will prove to be the only goal of the game against Manchester City at Maine Road. Nolberto Solano and Lomana LuaLua exchange passes on the right of the City box and

Solano works himself enough space to cross into the middle and Shearer heads past former Magpies keeper Tommy Wright (who had made a string of fine saves) at the far post to settle the match at Maine Road.

1 January 2007

David Edgar marks his Newcastle debut with the goal that earns the Magpies a 2-2 draw against Manchester United. Though James Milner had put the Toon ahead, two Paul Scholes goals either side of half-time had given the Reds a 2-1 lead. But Edgar decides to take matters into his own hands as he moves into the Manchester United half before taking a speculative shot that clips Scholes and just evades the dive of Edwin van der Sar to level the scores.

75

30 March 1974

United score a second goal in the 1974 FA Cup semi-final against Burnley at Hillsborough to all but seal a place at Wembley. With the Clarets putting the Magpies under increasing pressure, another attack is scrambled clear and the ball is cleared out to Terry Hibbitt on the left flank. Hibbitt hits a sublime first-time half-volley into the path of Malcolm Macdonald who races clear of his marker to tuck the ball through the keeper's legs and send more than 25,000 Newcastle fans wild in the process. It is Supermac's 23rd of another prolific campaign and it is enough to secure a thrilling 2-0 victory.

17 March 1984

A sublime chip by Terry McDermott puts Newcastle 2-1 up at home to Middlesbrough at St James' Park. Chris Waddle drifts into the Boro box before seeing a shot blocked but the ball comes to McDermott on the edge of the box who dinks a delightful shot over the keeper and into the far left-hand corner of the net to finally put the Magpies ahead. It is the former Liverpool midfielder's sixth of the campaign.

3 September 1993

Sub Alex Mathie makes an impact not long after coming on against Sheffield Wednesday at St James' Park.

Trailing 2-1, United attack as Barry Venison sends a ball towards Mathie in the box and his attempt to tee up a shot for a team-mate is blocked, but the quick-thinking youngster then attempts a chip into the middle where Rob Lee brings the ball down and Andy Cole spins to fire a low shot past Kevin Pressman and make it 2-2.

21 August 1994

The Magpies seal three impressive points as they go 3-0 up away to Leicester City. A poor clearance lands at the feet of Ruel Fox who spots sub Robbie Elliott's dash into the box and clips a cross to the left, where Elliott meets the ball on the half-volley to fire a low shot just inside the right-hand post and complete a deserved win for Kevin Keegan's side.

31 October 2010

Sunderland's Halloween horror is complete as Kevin Nolan scores his third and Newcastle's fifth during a memorable Tyne–Wear derby. With Black Cats fans already leaving St James' Park in their droves, Joey Barton's corner is flicked on by Shola Ameobi and Nolan heads home from close range to cap an unforgettable hat-trick for the skipper and make the score 5-0.

29 October 2014

Moussa Sissoko sends the Newcastle fans wild with delight as he creates and scores United's second – and decisive – goal against Manchester City. With a League

Cup quarter-final up for grabs, Magpies fans had travelled to Manchester in hope more than expectation, having failed to win in any of their previous 12 attempts at the Etihad. But with Newcastle leading 1-0, Sissoko effectively puts the game to bed as he pushes the ball past two City defenders on the edge of the box before beating Willy Caballero with a deft flick as the City keeper raced out. Thirteenth time lucky, then!

76

16 November 1974

Malcolm Macdonald gets the first of two late goals as the Magpies run riot at St James' Park. An incisive move through the centre of the park sees Tommy Cassidy nutmeg a Chelsea defender before feeding a ball in front of Supermac who rifles a right-foot shot past the keeper to make it 3-0 and seal two points.

18 October 1992

Newcastle make it 12 wins from 12 games to create history in the process. Having just been pegged back to 1-1 by Sunderland at Roker Park, United are awarded a free kick on the edge of the Sunderland box. Though four players stand over the ball, they part to let Liam O'Brien step up and curl a sublime right-foot free kick past the keeper from 20 yards out to send the travelling Toon Army wild behind the goal. It also secures a 2-1 win – a first success on Wearside for 36 long years.

8 January 1994

Another sublime Peter Beardsley goal seals passage into the FA Cup fourth round. Leading 1-0 against Coventry City at St James' Park, United finally put the game to bed as neat skills by Rob Lee see the former Charlton Athletic man play a ball into the path of

Beardsley who darts forward and skips past a defender into the box before gently lifting the ball over the keeper to make it 2-0 and settle the tie.

12 March 1994

A delightful piece of skill ends with the Magpies taking a 5-0 lead over Swindon Town at St James' Park. It is also a third goal in nine second-half minutes as the visitors wave the white flag, though this is arguably the pick of the bunch so far as Ruel Fox plays a low pass into the box and the feet of Steve Watson. Surrounded by defenders, Watson rolls his foot over the ball, taking him away from his markers, and then fires a powerful shot home from the corner of the six-yard box. A terrific piece of technique and finish.

12 February 2000

Alan Shearer doubles the Magpies' lead with a vital second goal against Manchester United. The visitors – reduced to ten men when Roy Keane is sent off – fail to clear the danger and Shearer collects the ball midway inside the United half. The England skipper moves towards goal and with nobody closing him down, lets fly with a low shot from 25 yards that beats Mark Bosnich and nestles in the bottom-right corner of the net to send St James' Park wild.

77

9 September 1972

David Craig scores the goal that seals a 2-1 victory over Arsenal at a sunny St James' Park. Ray Kennedy had pegged back the Magpies with an equaliser early in the second half but a Malcolm Macdonald long throw causes confusion in the Gunners' defence and the ball is only partially cleared as far as Craig who hits a swerving drive from 25 yards – the keeper gets it all wrong, perhaps caught in two minds, and the ball hits his hands and goes into the net.

17 March 1984

A delightful sweeping move sees United score a second goal in the space of three minutes to lead 3-1 against Middlesbrough. Peter Beardsley flicks the ball to Kevin Keegan who beats his man before sweeping the ball left for Kenny Wharton on the left flank – Wharton sizes up his options before sending a cross towards the far post where Keegan, who has by that point sprinted into the six-yard box, arrives in time to head the ball into the middle of the goal where defender Tony Mowbray can only help it over the line. It is Keegan's 23rd goal of a fantastic campaign.

23 February 1994

Andy Cole completes his hat-trick to wrap up three points and end a run of four successive losses in all competitions for Newcastle. Robbie Elliott rescues a seemingly lost cause when he retrieves possession on the left of the Coventry City box – his cross into the middle is cleared, but only as far as Peter Beardsley who jinks past one challenge then toe-pokes the ball through the legs of another defender and into the path of Cole who drills a low shot into the bottom-left corner of the net to make it 3-0 on the night. It is the fourth treble of the campaign and takes his tally in all competitions to 33 with three months of the 1993/94 season still to play.

29 November 1995

Steve Watson's goal gives Newcastle a rare win at Anfield in the Coca-Cola Cup fourth-round tie against Liverpool. Watson, who had scored a last-minute winner in the Premier League meeting at the start of November, again scored the winner against the Reds to put United into the last eight of the competition for the first time in 20 years and eliminate the holders in the process. Watson came off the bench after a head injury to Les Ferdinand and, on 77 minutes, he settled the tie in spectacular fashion. There seemed little on when Watson received Peter Beardsley's pass some 30 yards out, especially as there were three Liverpool defenders in front of him. Watson remained patient before making a yard of space for himself and chipping the ball over

David James to send the thousands of travelling Toon fans wild. It was only Liverpool's fourth home defeat ever in the League Cup but United's reward was a tough-looking trip to Arsenal in the quarter-finals.

1 January 1997

The Alan Shearer and Les Ferdinand show continues with the 25th goal between them in just 19 games. Having been denied a possible penalty after Shearer had been clearly brought down by keeper Nigel Martyn on the edge of the Leeds box, there is a sense of justice around St James' Park as the Magpies get the second goal their pressure merits. Peter Beardsley again picks out the head of Ferdinand who nods the ball towards Shearer who, with his back to goal, spins around and hits a shot that clips the heel of Carlton Palmer on its way past a wrong-footed Martyn to make it 2-0.

2 February 1997

Having led 1-0 after just three minutes, the Magpies find themselves 3-1 down after Leicester City score three goals in 13 second-half minutes. United begin their own 13-minute blitz in the shape of a thunderous Alan Shearer free kick into the roof of the net from 20 yards that the Foxes keeper does well to get out of the way from.

6 November 2002

United get back on level terms against Everton in the

League Cup tie at St James' Park. Hugo Viana's superb through ball for Kieron Dyer sees the England winger presented with a one-on-one chance with Richard Wright and Dyer toe-pokes the ball under the former Ipswich and Arsenal keeper to make it 1-1.

78

1 October 1997

Steve Watson's long throw-in results in United halving the deficit away to Dynamo Kyiv in the Group C Champions League clash in Ukraine. The Magpies had found themselves 2-0 down with just 28 minutes played thanks to goals from Sergei Rebrov and Andriy Shevchenko, but Kenny Dalglish's side dig in and stay in the game so, when Watson's throw causes confusion in the Kyiv box, John Beresford's low drive squeezes through the keeper's body to make it 2-1 in Kyiv's favour – but with 12 minutes left, there's still enough time to take something back to the north-east ...

19 September 1999

Any thoughts Sheffield Wednesday had that the Magpies – leading 5-0 from the 46th minute – had taken their foot off the gas are scuppered as United score their sixth of the afternoon. It comes from a Nolberto Solano corner as the Peruvian whips in a cross from the right and Gary Speed rises to thump a header home via the woodwork, though the Owls' misery is still not yet complete ...

6 November 2002

Kieron Dyer turns the League Cup tie with Everton on its head with a second goal in as many minutes.

Having trailed 1-0 to the Toffees up to the 77th minute, Dyer's equaliser gave the Magpies renewed energy and in the next attack, Carl Cort's neat lay-off is smashed home by Dyer to make it 2-1 and seemingly knocks the stuffing out of the visitors ... but the game will go into extra time as Everton find a late equaliser through David Unsworth's 89th-minute leveller.

79

4 January 1994

Robbie Elliott's slide rule pass sets Andy Cole clear to score the goal that seals three points for Kevin Keegan's side. With the clash with Norwich City at Carrow Road seemingly heading for a draw, Elliott plays Cole in and as the keeper comes out he skips around the challenge and knocks into the empty net to secure an excellent 2-1 win in East Anglia.

12 March 1994

Steve Watson scores his second goal in three minutes as United's rout of Swindon Town continues. Despite United scoring five already, the headlines looked more likely to be that the prolific Andy Cole wasn't among the scorers, but as the ball is played to Cole's feet inside the box, he spins and fires a low shot that the keeper pushes out, but only into the path of Watson who buries the shot into the back of the net from six yards out to make the score 6-1. It's just not Cole's day!

28 December 1996

Having looked as though they'd declared at 4-0, suddenly the goals start to flow again for the Magpies against Spurs. A crisp passing move eventually sees the ball played to the unmarked Philippe Albert on the edge of the Spurs box – he controls the pass and with just Ian Walker in net to beat, hits a low shot that the Tottenham No.1 makes a terrible hash of and allows to squeeze under his body to put United five goals to the good.

13 September 2016

A goal created by one centre-back and scored by another completes the rout over QPR at Loftus Road for the rampant Magpies. Ciaran Clark gets into the box on the left and crosses low into the middle where his defensive partner Grant Hanley calmly strokes the ball into the bottom-left corner to make it 6-0 and put Rafa Benitez's side into second place in the Championship.

80

26 December 2013

Papiss Cisse completes Stoke City's miserable trip to St James' Park with the fifth goal of the afternoon. Hatem Ben Arfa is brought down by Erik Pieters and the referee points to the penalty spot for the second time in the match. With Loic Remy missing a spot kick in the first half, Cisse steps up and emphatically thumps the ball into the top-right corner to make it 5-1 and keep the Magpies in touch with the Premier League pacesetters.

29 January 2019

Sean Longstaff catches Fernandinho in possession in his own box and the Manchester City defender's attempt at redemption sees Longstaff fouled and a penalty awarded. Matt Ritchie steps up to drill a low shot under the dive of Ederson and scores what will prove to be the winning goal against the defending Premier League champions and a priceless 2-1 victory. It also ends a miserable Magpies run against City that had seen 22 matches without a league win.

81

16 November 1974

Stewart Barrowclough compounds Chelsea's misery at St James' Park on a woeful day for the Londoners. The Magpies winger picks up possession on the right flank and then skips past a defender before drilling a low shot that seems to go through the goalkeeper and into the back of the net to make it 4-0 – much to the delight of the Gallowgate End.

14 February 1976

Future Bolton Wanderers player Alan Gowling gives United a 3-2 lead at Burnden Park in the FA Cup fifth round. Tommy Cassidy receives the ball 25 yards from goal and Gowling, who has managed to get behind the Bolton defence but has stayed onside, points to where he wants the ball. Cassidy obliges, plays a short pass into space and Gowling kicks the ball past the keeper from ten yards to score what seems like the winner – though the hosts score a late equaliser to force a St James' Park replay.

10 December 1988

A superb individual goal by John Hendrie seals a much-needed 2-1 win for the Magpies over Wimbledon. With United rooted to the foot of the table, victory in Jim

Smith's first home game in charge was crucial and Hendrie, who opened the scoring in the first half, wins the game as he collects the ball on the right flank and heads towards the Dons' box – he then cuts inside before swerving a low shot with the outside of his right boot to make it 2-1 and give the Toon Army a glimmer of hope that relegation might still be avoided.

3 September 1993

Substitute Alex Mathie marks his debut with a spectacular volley against Sheffield United as the Magpies come from behind to lead at St James' Park. Mathie, who had played a big part in Andy Cole's equaliser six minutes earlier, makes an intelligent run into the Owls' box and Malcolm Allen's chipped pass falls at a decent height for Mathie to slide and connect deftly to send the ball over Chris Woods and into the net. A superb strike by the 24-year-old Scot.

8 November 1993

Persistence and determination sees Andy Cole seal three points for the Magpies away to Oldham Athletic. When the ball is played into Cole's feet inside the Latics' box, he is at first foiled by a challenge – but he regains possession, spins around and fires a low shot into the bottom-left corner of the net to make it 3-1 and seal victory for United.

24 February 1996

Newcastle's man-of-the-match Philippe Albert drills home a low drive which is deflected off Niall Quinn and into the net for his second of the game and the sixth of a breath-taking afternoon as the Magpies come back to claim a 3-3 draw with relegation-threatened Manchester City at Maine Road.

19 September 1999

Alan Shearer bags his fourth of the game to make it a magnificent seven for the Magpies against Sheffield Wednesday. Arguably the scrappiest of the goals scored that day, another Nolberto Solano corner is crossed in and as the keeper flaps at his attempt to clear, the ball falls to Shearer who calmly side-foots a shot back past the hapless Owls custodian to make it 7-0.

11 April 2009

Andy Carroll gets the first goal of the Alan Shearer era as he levels to earn a point away to Stoke City. With Newcastle trailing 1-0 in Shearer's second game in charge, Carroll comes off the bench to rescue a point for his boyhood idol as he meets Damien Duff's cross with a header that loops over Potters keeper Thomas Sorensen to earn United a crucial point in the battle against relegation.

9 March 2019

Miguel Almiron fires a meaty drive from 30 yards that Everton keeper Jordan Pickford can only push into the path of Ayoze Perez who drills the ball home from close range to make it 2-2 at St James' Park and set up a grandstand finish to a game the Magpies had earlier trailed 2-0 in.

82

28 December 1996

A lovely team goal puts Newcastle 6-0 up against Tottenham at St James' Park – and deservedly so. David Batty crosses in from the left flank and, though the cross is behind Alan Shearer, Rob Lee stretches out his leg and directs the ball back into Shearer's path and he buries a shot past Ian Walker to almost complete Tottenham's misery – almost, but not quite!

15 September 2001

A wonderful Craig Bellamy burst forward sees the Welsh forward speed past a couple of Manchester United players and, as he approaches the box, he spots Nolberto Solano free on the edge of the area and plays him in, but his weak shot is cleared to the edge of the box where Alan Shearer drills a low drive that manages to find its way into the net from 18 yards out and restore the Magpies' lead. Having seen a 3-1 advantage disappear, Shearer's goal – later credited as a Wes Brown own goal – will secure a 4-3 victory for Sir Bobby Robson's men in a pulsating Premier League encounter with the Premier League champions at St James' Park.

22 March 2007

Michael Owen finally gets the goal that kills off Fulham's challenge and seals a first victory in 15 games for Kevin Keegan's men. The Magpies, desperate to kick-start their fight against relegation, had gone ahead after just six minutes against the Cottagers, but with tension and nervousness filtering down from the stands at St James' Park, Owen leaps to head past Kasey Keller to seal three welcome points and give Keegan his first win in 11 matches since returning to the hot seat on Tyneside.

83

23 April 1910

Jock Rutherford heads home a late equaliser to force an FA Cup Final replay with Barnsley. The Tykes had led from the 37th minute in the game played at Crystal Palace in London but the Magpies' dream of winning on their first FA Cup Final appearance lives on, much to the delight of a good proportion of the 77,747 crowd.

26 April 1924

Neil Harris dramatically breaks the deadlock in the 1924 FA Cup Final against Aston Villa. Dubbed the 'Rainy Day' final owing to the wet weather that plagued the 91,695 crowd, Harris's goal looks like proving the winner on the Magpies' first visit to Wembley Stadium, which had only opened for business a year earlier. But it won't be the end of the scoring in this game ...

29 May 1969

United take a commanding 3-0 lead in the Inter-Cities Fairs Cup Final first leg against Ujpest Dozsa with a wonderful goal, crafted by Jim Scott. There seems little danger for the Hungarians when Scott collects the ball on the left flank, but he shimmies past one challenge and then plays a short pass to the feet of Preben Arentoft who flicks a return ball into the path of Scott

– it looks slightly overhit but Scott just nips in ahead of the keeper to poke the ball home and send St James' Park into raptures.

1 October 1988

Newcastle's wretched run at Anfield finally comes to an end with a late Mirandinha winner. Dave Beasant's huge kick upfield is chased into the box by John Hendrie but he is tugged back by Gary Gillespie, leaving the referee no other option but to award a penalty. Brazilian striker Mirandinha is calmness personified as he strolls up and then sends the keeper the wrong way before celebrating in front of The Kop. The goal secures a 2-1 win over Liverpool for the struggling Magpies and ends a 38-year wait for victory at Anfield, easing the pressure on manager Willie McFaul – on his 45th birthday!

20 October 1996

The fifth Newcastle goal of the game and arguably the pick of the bunch. With the Magpies tearing Manchester United apart and attacking incessantly, a slow build-up on the right sees the ball played to Philippe Albert 15 yards outside the Manchester United box – with space to run and shoot, the Belgian bursts towards goal as if to hit a powerful shot goalwards, but as he pulls the trigger, he deftly lifts a chip over the United defenders and Peter Schmeichel – all of whom had been expecting a shot – and the ball instead drifts over all of them and under the crossbar to make it 5-0 for Kevin Keegan's side. Sublime and exquisite.

2 February 1997

Alan Shearer bags his second in six minutes to put the Magpies level at 3-3 with Leicester City. Faustino Asprilla finds Les Ferdinand who then plays a ball to the feet of Shearer who tees himself up before drilling a low shot through the legs of a Leicester defender and into the bottom-left corner of the net to set up a grandstand finish.

19 September 1999

Alan Shearer, who had previously never scored more than three goals in one game during his career, bags his fifth of the match against Sheffield Wednesday to complete a miserable afternoon for Danny Wilson's shell-shocked side. Paul Robinson is felled in the box by a lazy attempt at a tackle from a Wednesday player and Shearer drills a powerful penalty into the bottom-left corner to make it 8-0 and round off an incredible first home game in charge for Sir Bobby Robson and an incredible day for Magpies legend Shearer.

22 December 1999

Alan Shearer finishes what he had started as he puts United 5-1 up at St James' Park. As a ball is played to Shearer by Temuri Ketsbaia near the penalty spot, he swings to connect with the ball but has his shirt tugged back by a Spurs defender as he attempts to shoot. It's a clear penalty and Shearer dispatches the spot kick from more or less the same place he would have probably scored from anyway to make it 5-1 and guarantee a place in the FA Cup fourth round.

30 March 2007

Delight for the Magpies who are playing as though a huge weight has been lifted. Having ended a run of 14 games without victory a week earlier, United are 3-1 up away to Spurs and cruising – and any doubts about claiming their first back-to-back wins since December are ended when Joey Barton wins possession just outside his own box and immediately sends a pass to Obafemi Martins on the halfway line. Martins heads for goal, and turns Teemu Tainio inside out before drilling a low shot to Paul Robinson's right to complete a superb 4-1 win at White Hart Lane.

20 March 2016

Aleksandar Mitrovic rescues a point for Newcastle against Sunderland in the Tyne–Wear derby at St James' Park. Georgi Wijnaldum runs into space on the right and receives the ball. He looks up for options before deciding to take the left-back on and then float a deep cross to the back post where Mitrovic rises to head past the keeper from a tight angle and level the score at 1-1. Mitrovic's exuberant celebration matches those in the stands in a game United dare not lose. It is also the first goal scored under the Rafa Benitez era, with the Spanish boss having replaced Steve McClaren just nine days before.

9 March 2019

United complete a superb comeback as Ayoze Perez scores his second goal in three minutes to put the Magpies 3-2 up against Everton. Isaac Hayden knocks a clearance up high into the Everton box and with the Merseysiders' defence all at sea, Salomon Rondon brings the ball down with his thigh but, before he can shoot, Perez hits the ball past Jordan Pickford from close range to seal three points and send St James' Park wild.

84

26 April 1924

United score a second goal in two minutes to secure a second FA Cup success. Newcastle having only just gone ahead against Aston Villa at Wembley, the ball falls to Stan Seymour who unleashes a thunderous 20-yard volley past Villa keeper Tommy Jackson to make it 2-0 and end the Birmingham side's hopes once and for all. Soggy but with spirits high, the large contingent from the north-east celebrate long into the night as they make their way home. Seymour will go on to manage Newcastle United and later become chairman at St James' Park during an association that stretched over almost 60 years.

12 March 1994

The rout of Swindon Town ends with goal number seven, six minutes from time, at St James' Park. Rob Lee gets in space on the right of the box and his low cross into the middle is turned home by Ruel Fox to make it 7-1 and equal the Premier League record for the biggest win – shared with Blackburn Rovers. A memorable day for the home support, courtesy of Kevin Keegan's 'Entertainers'.

21 October 1995

Newcastle's 6-1 rout over ten-man Wimbledon is completed with the goal of the game from Philippe Albert. The Belgian defender runs on to a pass into the box on the left and clips a powerful left-foot shot in off the far-right post past makeshift goalkeeper Vinnie Jones before sprinting off in celebration – a sumptuous finish from the attack-minded defender.

85

12 May 1984

Peter Beardsley scores his 20th league goal of the season to round off a memorable final day of the 1983/84 campaign. Not only was it a promotion party with United already assured of a place back in the top flight, but it also Kevin Keegan's final game before retirement – and inevitably, the Magpies' crowd idol plays a part in the goal that secures victory over Brighton & Hove Albion, driving forward and finding Beardsley, whose first shot is blocked but, as the ball comes back to him, he immediately dinks a chip over the keeper from 20 yards to make it 3-1 and cap a wonderful day at a packed St James' Park.

26 October 1988

Mirandinha caps a superb performance with his second of the night to wrap up three crucial points for the Magpies. Leading 2-0 against in-form Middlesbrough, nails were still being bitten with 85 minutes on the clock, but when a ball is played into the path of the Brazilian striker, his pace takes him clear of Tony Mowbray and Gary Pallister before poking a shot at the keeper. The effort is saved but not held and Mirandinha is first to the loose ball, prodding it home to make it 3-0 and lift United off the foot of the table – at least for the time being.

22 December 1993

Andy Cole rescues a point for the Magpies with a superb individual goal. With Newcastle trailing 1-0 at home to Leeds United and with just five minutes remaining, Paul Bracewell pumps a long diagonal ball to the left corner of the Leeds box – Cole expertly brings down the ball and spins around to take on a defender. He holds it, nudges it along – then a bit more and, despite the presence of four Leeds players in front of him, finds enough space to fire a low right-foot shot through a crowd of legs from 20 yards and into the bottom corner to make it 1-1.

1 October 1997

After a late rally that had Dynamo Kyiv rocking, United force a late equaliser in the Champions League clash in Ukraine. A Keith Gillespie corner is not dealt with by the Kyiv defence and as Newcastle keep the pressure on, the ball falls to John Beresford 20 yards out – the Magpies defender had already scored seven minutes earlier and unleashes a volley that takes a sizeable deflection off Oleksandr Golovko and completely wrong-foots the keeper before bouncing inside the left post for a dramatic late equaliser and a precious 2-2 draw.

22 December 1999

Alan Shearer rounds off a superb FA Cup third-round replay as he emphatically heads home his second goal in three minutes. Shearer rises to power home Temuri Ketsbaia's excellent cross from six yards as United complete a 6-1 thrashing of Spurs at St James' Park.

24 May 2015

The goal that confirms Premier League survival also almost lifts the roof off St James' Park. The hugely popular Jonas Gutierrez – who had missed much of the season recovering from testicular cancer – moves purposefully towards the West Ham box before striking a low angled shot that beats the keeper and nestles in the bottom-left corner of the net. The celebrations are because United have relegated Hull City – in revenge for six years earlier – but also for the Gutierrez and his return to fitness.

86

11 May 1968

Though Newcastle had swapped blows with Division One leaders Manchester City in the first half and gone in 2-2 at the break, City, needing a victory to win only their second top-flight title, earn themselves breathing space with goals from Neil Young and Francis Lee. But the Magpies set up a nail-biting finish for the thousands of travelling fans inside St James' Park as the excellent Bryan Robson – a thorn in City's side throughout and scorer of two excellent goals – gets away down the left before sending a cross into the box where John McNamee heads powerfully past Ken Mulhearn to make it 4-3 in City's favour. With no further scoring, City hold on to win the title as news comes through that their closest rivals Manchester United have lost at home to Sunderland. The Magpies finish a respectable tenth in the table despite the loss.

25 April 1992

David Kelly scores a crucial winner to give Kevin Keegan's side a 1-0 win over Portsmouth as the Magpies desperately try to avoid a first-ever demotion to the Third Division. The only goal of a tense game – United's penultimate of the 1991/92 season – comes when Ray Ranson pumps a long ball to the edge of the

Pompey box for Mick Quinn to hook into the path of Kelly who fires a powerful rising shot across the keeper and into the left of the goal to send St James' Park wild.

23 February 1994

Sub Alex Mathie wraps up a 4-0 win for the Magpies at St James' Park. Mathie nudges the ball to Peter Beardsley on the halfway line and the Magpies' playmaker returns the pass by setting Mathie clear on goal and, as he enters the Coventry City box, he hits a low shot that the onrushing keeper Steve Ogrizovic gets something on but can't prevent from crossing the line to end a miserable trip to the north-east for the Sky Blues.

12 February 2000

A swift counter-attack sees Newcastle go 3-0 up against Manchester United at St James' Park and seal three points against Alex Ferguson's side. It starts with a neat piece of skill by Helder who casually knocks the ball over the head of a Manchester United attacker before finding Didier Domi on the left. Domi races towards the Reds' box before playing a precision pass into the area for Alan Shearer, who sweeps home from eight yards to confirm victory and preserve the Magpies' six-month unbeaten run at St James' Park.

1 December 2002

The greatest goal ever seen at St James' Park? Probably ... With United trailing 1-0 and just a few minutes remaining, ten-man Everton look set to head back to Merseyside with all three points – except they hadn't counted on a crazy last few minutes. The Toon Army are left rubbing their eyes as Laurent Robert's long pass finds Shola Ameobi on the edge of the Toffees' box – he heads to his left towards Shearer who waits for the ball to come down before unleashing a stunning angled volley that rockets into the top-right corner of the net from 25 yards out. It was, quite simply, magnificent.

11 May 2009

Peter Lovenkrands seals what will be Alan Shearer's only victory in charge of United. Leading 2-1 against Middlesbrough, the Magpies seal victory as Kevin Nolan's cross is swept home by Lovenkrands to make it 3-1 and all but guarantee three priceless points. Lovenkrands, like the scorer of the second goal – Obafemi Martins – had come on as a second-half sub. Sadly, 1-0 defeats to both Fulham and Aston Villa in the last two games of the campaign seal United's fate and the club are relegated after a 16-year stay in the top division. Shearer steps aside as manager and Chris Hughton is placed back in the hot seat for the 2009/10 Championship campaign.

21 December 2013

Game, set and match at Selhurst Park as Hatem Ben Arfa puts the Magpies 3-0 up. After Shola Ameobi is pushed over in the box, it is Ben Arfa who steps up to convert the penalty and secure United's sixth win in eight games to move them to within six points of leaders Liverpool.

87

1 January 1997

What will be the last Premier League goal of Kevin Keegan's five-year spell as Newcastle boss seals a 3-0 win over Leeds United at St James' Park. It's a goal that has all the panache that entertained the Magpies' fans for much of his time as manager and begins with Peter Beardsley's clever cross from the left of the box for Rob Lee who holds off a challenge, turns around and then does a Cruyff Turn to leave his marker and whips a cross into the six-yard box where Les Ferdinand reacts quickest to force the ball home and complete a fully deserved victory. Though Keegan remained in charge for the away FA Cup tie with Charlton Athletic, he resigned shortly after, stating: 'It was my decision and my decision alone to resign. I feel I have taken the club as far as I can, and that it would be in the best interests of all concerned if I resigned now. I wish the club and everyone concerned with it all the best for the future.' It was the end of an era for the Toon.

17 April 2006

Albert Luque puts the cherry on the cake as he puts the Magpies 4-1 up at Sunderland. It is yet another Keystone Cops moment as two Sunderland players go for and miss a high ball on the halfway line and Luque races clear and draws the keeper off his line before lifting it over his dive to seal victory in emphatic style at the Stadium of Light.

22 August 2011

United go five goals up with another badly defended corner from Aston Villa. The visitors' misery is not quite over when Kevin Nolan finishes from close range to bag his second goal of the game at St James' Park.

88

16 November 1974

Malcolm Macdonald grabs his second and United's fifth as the Magpies complete a memorable day at St James' Park. Supermac receives the ball on the left of the Chelsea box before nutmegging a defender and firing a thunderous angled drive past the keeper to complete a 5-0 victory over the Londoners.

3 September 1993

Malcolm Allen scores his second of the season to seal a 4-2 win over Sheffield Wednesday at St James' Park. Having trailed 2-1 with 15 minutes to go, United complete a remarkable comeback as Rob Lee's whipped-in ball is glanced home by Allen on the edge of the six-yard box and secures only a second victory in the opening seven games of the 1993/94 season.

5 March 1994

Andy Cole grabs a last-gasp winner away to ten-man Sheffield Wednesday. The hosts are reduced in number when Cole, through on goal, is brought down by Owls defender Andy Pearce just outside the box and referee Paul Durkin deems the challenge to be a professional foul. From the resulting free kick, a low ball finds its way towards Ruel Fox, hitting the inside of his ankle and bouncing kindly into the path of Cole who bags his 34th of an incredible season with a shot from close range.

21 August 1996

Alan Shearer marks his home debut with the goal that seals a 2-0 victory over Wimbledon. Signed for a world-record £15m from Blackburn, it is the stuff of schoolboy dreams for the lifelong Magpies fan as he steps up to take a free kick slightly left of centre and some 25 yards out and then curls a superb shot into the top-right corner to nearly lift the roof off an ecstatic St James' Park. It is the first of 206 goals for United.

28 December 1996

Rob Lee caps a superb performance with his second – and Newcastle's seventh – as the Magpies complete the destruction of Tottenham at St James' Park. What will be the final home goal of a majestic attacking display by Kevin Keegan's men is the result of excellent approach play by David Batty, who exchanges passes with John Beresford before eventually laying a short ball to Rob Lee who strikes a low right-foot shot into the bottom-left corner of the net. The visitors score a consolation a minute later but head home having been spanked 7-1 in what – remarkably – would be Keegan's penultimate game as manager at St James' Park.

30 November 2019

United grab a late equaliser at St James' Park to further dent Manchester City's title hopes. Just ten months before, the Magpies had handed the initiative to Liverpool in the race for the title by beating City 2-1, and though this game will end in a draw, it is still two more points dropped for the Premier League's defending champions. With Newcastle awarded a free kick on the right of the City box, the City defenders prepare for a cross into the middle – but Christian Atsu instead rolls the free kick back to Jonjo Shelvey on the edge of the box and the former Swansea and Liverpool midfielder hits a sweet curling shot that flies past Brazilian keeper Ederson to make it 2-2.

89

17 December 1989

Super sub Michael O'Neill rescues a precious point for Newcastle with a late equaliser against Southampton. The Northern Ireland international had already halved the deficit earlier in the half when Glenn Roeder's ball out of defence is flicked on by Rob McDonald, and O'Neill does the rest, holding off a challenge on the left of the box before turning and firing a left-foot shot into the bottom-right corner to give the bottom of the table Magpies a precious 3-3 draw.

1 December 2002

St James' Park erupts as the Magpies score a second goal in three minutes to turn a 1-0 deficit against ten-man Everton into a 2-1 victory. With the stadium still rocking from Alan Shearer's world-class volley on 86 minutes, the Toffees concede a second and decisive goal. Craig Bellamy scampers down the right flank and into the Everton box, getting in behind the defence, and his low cross strikes Li Tie's foot and beats Richard Wright on his near post to win the game for United.

25 October 2004

Olivier Bernard refuses to concede defeat in a battle for possession on the left of Manchester City's box

– the French defender eventually wrestles free of the challenge before whipping a cross back into the middle where Craig Bellamy expertly diverts a volley into the bottom-right corner to make it 4-3 and seal a dramatic victory for the Magpies in what had been a seesaw battle between Graeme Souness's and Kevin Keegan's sides at St James' Park.

2 November 2013

Brilliant work by Vurnon Anita results in the second goal that finally seals victory for United against Jose Mourinho's Chelsea. With Newcastle having survived two near misses in the space of a few seconds at the other end, Anita shrugs off one challenge on the left of the box before cutting inside of another and pulling the ball back into the middle where Loic Remy strikes a crisp low shot first time that strikes the foot of the post and arrows into the opposite corner of the net to complete an impressive 2-0 victory at St James' Park.

90

4 May 1993

Game, set and match at Blundell Park as United seal the second-tier title and promotion back to the top flight by doubling their lead in the last minute. Andy Cole manages to knock a pass on and David Kelly takes over, racing through on goal before taking the ball around the keeper and slotting home despite the presence of two Grimsby Town defenders. The goal leads to scenes of jubilation among the thousands of travelling United fans who can now celebrate a well-deserved title success.

19 March 1994

Alex Mathie scores his third goal of the campaign from the bench to seal a 4-2 win away to West Ham. Inevitably, Peter Beardsley is the catalyst, scampering down the right flank and then going around full-back Tim Breacker before crossing low into the six-yard box where, after a blocked shot, the ball lands at the feet of Andy Cole – he nudges it to his right and Mathie's low angled shot finds the bottom-left corner of the net to ensure there is now no way back for the Hammers. It also gives Cole a rare hat-trick of assists to go with the goal he scored.

3 February 1996

A glorious passing move and period of keep-ball ends with United finally sealing a 2-0 win over Sheffield Wednesday. As the Magpies zip the ball around in the Owls' half, Peter Beardsley puts Lee Clark clear on the left of the Wednesday box and the midfielder draws the keeper before curling a right-foot shot into the far right of the net to seal three points and give Kevin Keegan's men a 13th straight home win to preserve their 100 per cent home record.

2 February 1997

Alan Shearer completes a 13-minute hat-trick as Newcastle come from 3-1 down with 77 minutes played to win 4-3. As Leicester attempt to play down the clock with the game in the final minute, Robbie Elliott plays a pass to Rob Lee inside the box and his low cross is turned in at the far post by Shearer to complete the most dramatic of comebacks at St James' Park.

15 September 2001

Alan Shearer stands his ground as Roy Keane loses his rag in an absorbing clash against Manchester United at St James' Park. With Newcastle leading 4-3, Shearer runs the ball into the corner before it crosses the line for a throw-in for the Reds. Shearer makes a nuisance of himself and Keane petulantly throws the ball at him. In the ensuing melee, Keane throws a punch at Shearer

– who doesn't flinch, and then watches with contempt as Keane is shown a red card.

22 July 2006

Emre caps a sparkling performance with a stunning goal. With United already assured of UEFA Cup qualification thanks to earlier goals from Shola Ameobi, the Turkish international collects a pass on the right of the Lillestrom box before dropping his left shoulder, jinking past a defender, and curling a left-foot shot into the top-left corner and making it 3-0. The Magpies win 4-1 on aggregate and progress to the UEFA Cup's early stages as a result.

22 September 2010

Shola Ameobi grabs a dramatic late winner for United to seal a thrilling 4-3 victory at Stamford Bridge. The Magpies had led 3-1, but Chelsea had fought back and Nicolas Anelka's 87th-minute penalty levelled the scores and then the hosts had rattled the woodwork! The equaliser had looked like forcing extra time, but undeterred, United win a corner in the final minute. Jonas Gutierrez sends in the corner from the left and Ameobi makes a superb run towards the left corner of the six-yard box, losing marker Bruma in the process, and gets the perfect connection to head the ball past keeper Ross Turnbull and into the right corner of the net and send Newcastle into the fourth round of the League Cup. A superb win and a fantastic game of football for the travelling Toon Army who were there in their thousands as usual.

4 January 2012

United keeper Tim Krull claims a rare assist as Manchester United's misery is completed at St James' Park. With Newcastle already 2-0 up at a buoyant St James' Park, Krull pumps a long ball into the Manchester United half and, as it lands in the United box, Phil Jones – unaware of where his keeper is – desperately tries to head the ball down into the turf and, in doing so, directs it past David de Gea to make it 3-0 against the defending Premier League champions.

2 February 2013

Moussa Sissoko's dream home debut is capped by a second goal – and this is a last-gasp winner against Chelsea. Sissoko plays a part in the move that leads to the goal, finding Davide Santon in space on the left and then receiving the ball back on the edge of the box before hitting a first-time low drive past an unsighted Petr Cech to send St James' Park wild. It's a dream start to life in the north-east for the £1.5m signing from Toulouse and gives the Magpies three vital points.

12 January 2016

Newcastle snatch a last-gasp point against Manchester United in a thrilling St James' Park encounter. United had twice led – 2-0 and 3-2 – when the Magpies launch one last sortie on the Reds' defence. Daryl Janmaat picks up a loose ball on the right of the box, puts a cross in towards Aleksandar Mitrovic and the partial clearance falls to Paul Dummett who arrives like a steam train to thump a ferocious drive into the roof of the net from 12 yards out to earn a dramatic 3-3 draw.

7 May 2017

Just as news is filtering through that Brighton had conceded an 89th-minute Jack Grealish goal away to Aston Villa, United get the third goal that effectively ends the game and wins the Championship for the Magpies. On a special day for Rafa Benitez's men, Aleksandar Mitrovic puts Dwight Gayle through and the former Crystal Palace striker – on his first game back after missing most óf April with injury – calmly slots home past the Barnsley keeper to make it 3-0 and spark joyous celebrations around St James' Park as the news that Brighton's game had ended 1-1 was confirmed shortly after.

12 May 2019

Popular striker Salomon Rondon completes a 4-0 win for United away to Fulham. The on-loan forward hits a low shot that is pushed out by keeper Sergio Rico but only back into the path of Rondon who makes no mistake with his second effort in what will be Rafa Benitez's final game in charge of the Magpies.

90+2

15 May 2011

United grab an injury-time equaliser to deny Chelsea victory, though the London side's title hopes had already ended a few weeks before. In the penultimate game of the 2010/11 campaign, the resilient Magpies level for the second time in the game. Ryan Taylor – who had scored in the first half – whips in a corner that Nile Ranger flicks on and Steven Taylor heads home at the far post to earn a creditable 2-2 draw at Stamford Bridge against the Premier League runners-up.

90+3

2 May 1992

Newcastle grab a dramatic late winner to seal survival on the last day of the 1991/92 campaign. Kevin Keegan's arrival in February had turned United's fortunes around and they travelled to Filbert Street against promotion-chasing Leicester on the final day looking to avoid defeat to stay in the division. Despite the Magpies going in 1-0 up at the break, the Foxes levelled through Steve Walsh on 90 minutes. But in a bizarre twist, Walsh would make it two goals in a few minutes as he inadvertently pokes the ball past his own keeper, chasing a long clearance back towards his own goal. The 2-1 win confirms United's survival and the Keegan era begins in earnest ...

22 August 2011

Andy Carroll completes his hat-trick on a memorable opening home game of the campaign for the Magpies. Xisco turns away from one challenge before slipping an inviting through ball for Carroll who – clear on goal – controls the pass before tucking a low left-foot drive past Brad Friedel.

90+4

2 May 2012

A contender for goal of the decade, never mind season, as Papiss Cisse's red-hot form seals a 2-0 victory over Chelsea at Stamford Bridge. A throw-in on the left finds Shola Ameobi who chests the ball to Cisse on the left corner of the Chelsea box – the Senegal striker immediately half-volleys a swerving, angled shot with the outside of his right boot that flies like a missile over Petr Cech and into the roof of the far right of the net. An absolutely stunning strike from a player who – with 13 goals in 12 games – was in the form of his life. An outrageous effort.

18 January 2020

United move seven points clear of the relegation zone with a last-gasp winner against Chelsea at St James' Park. Despite having been dominated by the visitors for long periods, the Magpies score the only goal of the game deep into added time when Allan Saint-Maximin's excellent cross from the left is glanced past Kepa by Isaac Hayden to give Steve Bruce's side three very welcome points.

21 January 2020

United, trailing 2-0, score what looks to be a consolation goal as Matt Ritchie's corner is palmed away by Jordan

Pickford — but only as far as Fabian Schar who sees his shot parried by Pickford to the edge of the six-yard box where sub Florian Lejeune acrobatically sends an overhead kick past the keeper and the defenders around him to halve the deficit.

90+5

28 September 2016

Trailing 3-2 and with added time almost up, the Magpies score a dramatic equaliser to lift the roof off St James' Park. DeAndre Yedlin provides the cross from the right and his ball into the middle finds Yoan Gouffran, who plants his header home from close range to seemingly salvage a point for Rafa Benitez's men – but remarkably, there is still just enough time for one final twist in this thrilling match ...

21 January 2020

With seconds remaining, United throw everything at Everton for one last attack, looking to complete a remarkable comeback. As the ball is pinged into the box by Matt Ritchie, it falls for Federico Fernandez on the right of the six-yard box. His shot thumps the post and rebounds into the middle of the box and, after a shot is blocked by Jordan Pickford, Florian Lejeune pokes the ball goalwards from close range – Pickford initially appears to have kept it out and the ensuing scramble ends with the ball in the keeper's arms. But goal-line technology correctly awards the goal as Pickford was well behind the line and the ball was just over – it means United had come from 2-0 down with 94 minutes played to score twice in 102 seconds and claim an incredible 2-2 draw.

90+6

28 September 2016

Just 59 seconds after equalising against Norwich, Dwight Gayle completes his hat-trick to win the game for the Magpies 4-3. It is an incredible finish to the game with Gayle holding off a challenge on the edge of the box and then firing past the keeper, resulting in wild celebrations around a disbelieving St James' Park. Though United had left it late, the fact they'd had 22 shots to Norwich's seven suggests justice was done in the end.

100

15 January 1997

Alan Shearer ensures new manager Kenny Dalglish's first game in charge ends in victory. The FA Cup third-round replay with Charlton Athletic goes into extra time at St James' Park when the Magpies are awarded a free kick some 30 yards from goal. With the Charlton focus seemingly on Les Ferdinand's movements in the box, Shearer hits a beautiful curling shot into the top-left corner to make it 2-1 and the goal will also prove to be the winner.

6 November 2002

In a topsy-turvy League Cup clash at St James' Park, United level for the second time of the night to make it 3-3 against Everton. Alessandro Pistone turns the ball past his own keeper to give the Magpies yet another lifeline, but with no further scoring the match is decided on penalties, with the visitors triumphing 3-2.

103

24 April 1974

Bobby Moncur scores the goal that wins United the Texaco Cup. Malcolm Macdonald had earlier equalised against Burnley but, in a closely fought game played in front of a crowd of 34,540, it is Moncur's strike that settles the game and brings the first silverware of the decade back to St James' Park – albeit not a major one.

104

1 October 1991

Having conceded two quick extra-time goals against Tranmere Rovers, United pull the score back to 5-4. Micky Quinn's pressing looks to end with a foul on the Tranmere defender, but the referee allows play to continue and Lee Clark slots a low drive from the edge of the box to keep the Magpies' hopes alive in the Zenith Data Systems Cup tie at Prenton Park.

105+3

15 January 2019

Deep into stoppage time of the first period of extra time, United regain the lead against Blackburn Rovers at Ewood Park. Looking marginally offside, the lack of VAR helps the Magpies as Joselu is the first to react after a powerful shot is fumbled by the Rovers keeper and the Spaniard reacts first, clipping the shot neatly home from eight yards to put Newcastle 3-2 up in the FA Cup third-round tie.

106

15 January 2019

United seal a place in the FA Cup fourth round by going 4-2 up against Blackburn Rovers at Ewood Park. In a swift counter-attack down the right, Joselu and Matt Ritchie combine to free Ayoze Perez who takes the ball into the box on the right, before dropping his shoulder and firing a fierce angled shot into the top-left corner of the net.

109

11 April 1999

Having escaped a clear handball in the first half in the box, Newcastle rub salt in the wounds of Tottenham Hotspur in the FA Cup semi-final clash at Old Trafford. With normal time ending 0-0, the Magpies attack and, as a ball is looped over Sol Campbell in the box, the Spurs defender instinctively puts his arm up and touches the ball with his hand. The referee points to the spot and Alan Shearer emphatically belts home the penalty, sending the keeper the wrong way in the process, to put United just ten minutes away from a second successive FA Cup Final.

110

1 October 1991

In a crazy but thoroughly entertaining Zenith Data Systems Cup tie away to Tranmere Rovers, Gavin Peacock bags his second of the night to make it 5-5. Robbie Elliott cleverly plays in Lee Clark and his cross into the six-yard box is turned home by Peacock for the tenth goal of the night at Prenton Park.

115

4 February 2020

Allan Saint-Maximin scores a superb individual goal to give the Magpies a dramatic extra-time winner against Oxford United. The hosts had looked dead and buried at 2-0 down with six minutes remaining, but two late goals forced the game into extra time and the match seemed to be heading to penalties when Saint-Maximin received the ball on the left, moved inside and went past two challenges before firing a ferocious left-foot shot home from 18 yards to win the FA Cup fourth-round tie and put United into the fifth round for the first time in 14 years.

116

7 November 2006

Skipper Scott Parker caps a superb display by scoring the goal that means a penalty shoot-out will be needed to determine the team who progresses into the League Cup quarter-finals. Watford had come from behind to lead 2-1 at Vicarage Road, but Parker races onto a fine Nolberto Solano pass before calmly slotting past Richard Lee to make it 2-2 deep into extra time.

118

1 October 1991

Drama in the closing stages of extra time in an absorbing Zenith Data Systems Cup tie as Alan Neilson bursts into the Tranmere Rovers box only to be felled by Graham Branch resulting in a penalty with just two minutes remaining. With Newcastle having trailed 5-3, Micky Quinn steps up to fire the ball past Eric Nixon and make it 6-5 – while also completing his hat-trick. Incredibly, John Aldridge will score his fourth of the game with virtually the last kick of the game to make it 6-6 and send the game to penalties where the Magpies' notorious shoot-out jinx strikes again as Rovers triumph 3-2 at Prenton Park.

11 April 1999

Alan Shearer sends half of Old Trafford wild with a truly stunning strike. With Newcastle leading 1-0 and with just a couple of minutes of the FA Cup semi-final remaining, the ball is played to Shearer on the right of the Spurs box and he unleashes a swerving right-foot shot that bends away from the keeper and into the top right of the net to seal a 2-0 win and a second successive FA Cup Final appearance – this time against Manchester United.

119

27 August 1997

With just a minute remaining of the Champions League second qualifying round, second leg tie away to Croatia Zagreb, the match looks to be heading for penalties. The home side had fought back from being a goal down and a man down to lead 2-1 and force extra time when all their hard work is undone by a simple passing move as David Batty finds Faustino Asprilla on the edge of the box and he plays it to his right where Georgian striker Temuri Ketsbaia arrives to drill the ball home from 12 yards. The goal means United win 4-3 on aggregate and qualify for the Champions League group stage.

Penalty shoot-outs

As the Magpies have only one successful shoot-out up to June 2020, we'll focus on the one that ended in victory ...

7 November 2006

Having drawn 2-2 with Watford, a penalty shoot-out ensued at the end of the League Cup tie at Vicarage Road.

Nolberto Solano (Newcastle United) – scores – 1-0

Darius Henderson (Watford) – scores – 1-1

James Milner (Newcastle United) – misses – 1-1

Ashley Young (Watford) – misses – 1-1

Emre (Newcastle United) – scores – 2-1

Matthew Spring – (Watford) – scores – 2-2

Damien Duff (Newcastle United) – scores – 3-2

Al Bangura (Watford) – scores – 3-3

Stephen Carr (Newcastle United) – scores – 4-3

Hameur Bouazza (Watford) – scores – 4-4

Charles N'Zogbia (Newcastle United) – scores – 5-4

Jordan Stewart – (Watford) – misses – 5-4

Newcastle United win 5-4 on penalties – the first penalty shoot-out victory in NUFC history up to that date in the Magpies' history!

Also available at all good book stores

9781785315534

9781785316838

9781785316258

9781785316326

9781785315411

9781785314384